THE AMERICAN NEGRO

HIS HISTORY AND LITERATURE

THE NEGRO MIGRANT
IN PITTSBURGH

Abraham Epstein

ARNO PRESS and THE NEW YORK TIMES

NEW YORK 1969

General Editor
WILLIAM LOREN KATZ

THE HISTORY OF MOST AMERICAN CITIES HAS BEEN SORELY neglected, and this is especially true of the Negro's part in that history. This short "study in social economics" by Abraham Epstein, focusing on the Pittsburgh of 1917 during the World War I industrial boom, should fill some of the gap and prove useful to the sociologist, social worker, historian, and labor economist. Not only is it a prime source of information and analysis on the problems confronting Negroes in their migration to the urban North, but it also represents an important kind of research which has been largely overlooked by the academic social sciences: urban studies supervised by college professors and conducted by students working cooperatively with local settlement houses and social workers. Epstein's study was fortunate enough to be published in pamphlet form, avoiding the dismal obscurity of most such studies.

The work is in the tradition of the monumental Pittsburgh Survey (1909–1914) directed by Paul U. Kellogg (which, oddly enough, Epstein fails to mention) and, before that, Charles Booth's *Labour of the People of London* (1903), and the inclusion of family budget data is reminiscent of Frederic Le Play's earlier studies of *The European Worker*. Like them, it combines statistics and case descriptions with a moral passion for alleviating human suffering. The comparison is only limited, of course; Epstein, who did the study while a graduate student at the University of Pittsburgh, completed it in little more than six months. It therefore lacks the elaborate trappings of more professional social research, but this only serves to make Epstein's achievement all the more impressive.

Considering that the study was published over a half-century ago, it stands the test of time remarkably well. To be sure, some of the author's reasoning is out-moded and unscientific— for example, his view that one of the reasons for higher Negro than white mortality rates is that "due to the climatic and environmental maladjustments, his racial power of resistance is not as great as that of the white"—but in general the research methods on infant mortality, early death, and high disease rates among Negroes, are quite sophisticated and show considerable ingenuity.

Epstein's interview schedule, used in over 500 interviews, yielded valuable demographic data on family status and size, housing conditions, employment, income, and the history of northward migration. His survey of major Pittsburgh industries clearly documents their resistance to hiring Negroes at any level of work. His careful marshaling of data to refute what he calls the "popular belief in a Negro 'wave of crime, rape and murder' " is handled well, although his argument would probably have been even stronger if he had used *conviction* rather than *arrest* statistics. Except for a few scientific errors and such curiosa as the table which notes that in one year eighteen Negro families had received charity for "sexual irregularity," eight for "begging tendency," and one for "hereditary pauperism," etc., many parts of the book could well have been written today, a compliment to Epstein's research, but an obvious indictment of the slow progress toward racial equality in America.

Only two examples are necessary to make this point. Now that the public schools are under attack for failing to educate the children of the poor, it is shocking to realize that what has recently been presented as startling major "new evidence" was recognized at least fifty years ago when Epstein wrote that "practically all school principals stated that in the first four years the Negro child keeps well up with its white school mates, but . . . after the fourth grade, the Negro child often falls behind and cannot keep up with the whites." What did these principals suggest? Vocational training! Why were the schools not adapted to the particular needs of the particular children? Epstein reports their explanation was that "in the formal character of the school curriculum they have little freedom to develop their own schemes." These rationalizations ring all too familiarly, for they are still with us in the current battle over community control of the schools.

Epstein's evidence in the field of labor and employment

also remains depressingly familiar. He reported that the excuse employers gave for not hiring and upgrading Negroes was that white workers would not work alongside them. He correctly notes that "while there is an undeniable hostility to Negroes on the part of a few white workers, the objection is frequently exaggerated by prejudiced gang bosses." Equally important, he documents the almost universal resistance of labor unions to accepting Negro members, and refutes the familiar charge that Negroes have been willing strikebreakers who are impossible to organize. He answers this argument with proof that, with very few exceptions, "none of the . . . Unions made any effort to organize the colored workers in their respective trades, and they cannot therefore complain of the difficulty of organizing the Negroes." His conclusion, *in 1917,* has been reiterated often in recent years: "If the present policy of the American labor movement continues, the Negroes can depend but little upon this great liberating force for their advancement." He adds, "the white laboring classes have to contend only with the manufacturers. The Negroes, however, have to contend with the white trade unions as well as with the employers."

These examples of Epstein's astute grasp of the social and economic realities of World War I Pittsburgh are intended only to whet the reader's appetite. They could easily be multiplied by the author's discussions of the relations between bad housing and health and social problems, or the motives for Negro migration to the North and the return trip South that many of them made, or the indifference of elected officials to the problems of poverty. Not the least of the book's virtues is Epstein's discernment in not labeling all problems affecting Negroes as "Negro problems;" instead, he makes the important distinction between "the Negro's Own Problem" and "the Community's Problem."

This document should win a permanent place on every Negro history shelf, and will provide new source material for urban sociology and the other urban behavioral sciences.

Arthur Jordan Field
DEPARTMENT OF HISTORY AND POLITICAL SCIENCE
RENSSELAER POLYTECHNIC INSTITUTE

A STUDY IN SOCIAL ECONOMICS

PUBLISHED UNDER THE SUPERVISION OF THE
SCHOOL OF ECONOMICS
UNIVERSITY OF PITTSBURGH

The Negro Migrant in Pittsburgh

BY

ABRAHAM EPSTEIN
B. S. in Economics

PRICE FIFTY CENTS

PITTSBURGH, PA.
1918

CONTENTS

PREFACE.

The main purpose of this study was not merely the attempt at a piece of research. The writer undertook it originally in the early spring as a student volunteer with the sole aim of doing his share in the development of a more virile civic consciousness in Pittsburgh, and to contribute something toward the orientation and adjustment of the newcomers in our community. Thanks to the generous cooperation of Mr. Walter A. May, the writer was enabled to devote all his time since June 1917 to the completion of this study. An attempt has been made to interpret the data from the social point of view. The conclusions are not offered as final but it is hoped they may serve as the basis for a practical community program and perhaps for further study.

The writer wishes to acknowledge his indebtedness to Prof. Francis D. Tyson for his counsel and assistance in planning and organizing this study. Without his cooperation, the study could not have been undertaken or completed. The writer also acknowledges his thanks to Mr. George M. P. Baird of the English Department, University of Pittsburgh for reading the manuscript and making many suggestions as to style. Much thanks is also due to Mr. Edmund Feldman for his valuable assistance in preparing the tables and making the graphs. To the Irene Kaufmann Settlement and its resident workers, the writer wishes to express his gratitude and appreciation for their cooperation and hospitality.

Pittsburgh, Pa.,   A. E.
December 1, 1917.

INTRODUCTION

This little study of the Negro Migration to Pittsburgh was first suggested as a thesis subject in a university class in Social Economy in May, 1917. Our great steel city of the North calls many unskilled workers to its mills. The migration of Negroes to fill the gaps in the ranks of this labor force, opened up by the cessation of European immigration following the war has been under way for nearly eighteen months. Expanding steel production continues to call for more workers. From the first labor agents of railroads and steel mills as well as private employment agencies have been at work gathering in the new army of laborers.

By last spring newspaper reports of housing congestion, and of suffering from pneumonia and other diseases, and tales of the increase of crime and vice were being spread. There was spoken comment of the new situation on every hand. But these reports were inaccurate; they gave no concrete estimate of the number and character of the newcomers; and no definite stateture of their life here or the problems of community adjustment created by the influx of strange people.

It is to be hoped that the attempt at an intensive and supervised investigation represented by these pages will prove of value to those members of both races who have already seen in the migration new opportunity for a people whose need has been bitter, as well as a chance for manifold human service. Perhaps the all-too-faulty product may justify the painstaking effort of the investigator who toiled through the hot summer months and the generosity of the public-spirited citizen whose interest made the study possible.

The report may be of value also in offering suggestions to those workers in other cities who are dealing with the same many-sided and baffling problem, so full of pathos and tragedy and so expressive of the need of community cooperation. At least they may avoid the pitfalls upon which we have stumbled. For Pittsburgh it may well be that the material gathered here will be used to assist in carrying forward a constructive program for adjusting the new workers permanently to our community life. Industrial production here in a time of crisis depends in part upon our Negro labor supply, the stability and efficiency of which can be permanently secured only by successful experiments in the fields of housing, health, and recreation.   **FRANCIS TYSON,**
University of Pittsburgh,   *Professor of Social Economy.*
December, 1917.

GENERAL CONDITIONS AMONG NEGRO MIGRANTS IN PITTSBURGH

Chapter I.

The Negro population of the Pittsburgh Districts in Allegheny County, was 27,753 in the year 1900 and had increased to 34,217 by the year 1910, according to the latest United States Census figures available.* The increase during this period was 23.3%. Assuming the continuation of this rate of increase, the total Negro population in 1915 would be about 38,000.

From a canvas of twenty typical industries in the Pittsburgh district, it was found that there were 2,550 Negroes employed in 1915, and 8,325 in 1917, an increase of 5,775 or 227%. It was impossible to obtain labor data from more than approximately sixty percent of the Negro employing concerns, but it is fair to assume that the same ratio of increase holds true of the remaining forty percent. On this basis the number of Negroes now employed in the district may be placed at 14,000. This means that there are about 9,750 more Negroes working in the district today than there were in 1915, an addition due to the migration from the South.

A schedule study of over five hundred Negro migrants indicates that thirty percent of the new comers have their families with them, and that the average family consists of three persons, excluding the father.** Adding to the total number of new workers, (9,750), the product obtained by multiplying thirty percent by three, (average family), we find a probable total new Negro population of 18,550 in 1917.

This sudden and abnormal increase in the Negro population within so short a time, of necessity involves a tremendous change, and creates a new situation, which merits the attention of the whole community. Before this great influx of Negroes from the South, the Negro population which constituted only 3.4% of the total city population, lived in a half dozen sections of the city. Although not absolutely segregated, these districts were distinct.

*13th U. S. Census, Penna. Bulletin, Table I, page 12; 1910.

**This average was obtained by dividing the total number of women and children of the families investigated, by the number of families.

Because of the high cost of materials and labor, incident to the war; because the taxation system still does not encourage improvements,[†] and because of investment attractions other than in realty, few houses have been built and practically no improvements have been made. This is most strikingly apparent in the poorer sections of the city. In the Negro sections, for instance, there have been almost no houses added and few vacated by whites within the last two years. The addition, therefore, of thousands of Negroes, just arrived from Southern states, meant not only the creation of new Negro quarters and the dispersion of Negroes throughout the city, but also the utmost utilization of every place in the Negro sections capable of being transformed into a habitation. Attics and cellars, store-rooms and basements, churches, sheds and warehouses had to be employed for the accommodation of these new-comers. Whenever a Negro had space which he could possibly spare, it was converted into a sleeping place; as many beds as possible were crowded into it, and the maximum number of men per bed were lodged. Either because their own rents were high, or because they were unable to withstand the temptation of the sudden, and, for all they knew, temporary harvest, or, perhaps because of the altruistic desire to assist their race fellows, a majority of the Negroes in Pittsburgh converted their homes into lodging houses.

Because rooms were hard to come by, the lodgers were not disposed to complain about the living conditions or the prices charged. They were only too glad to secure a place where they could share a half or at least a part of an unclaimed bed. It was no easy task to find room for a family, as most boarding houses would accept only single men, and refused to admit women and children. Many a man, who with his family occupied only one or two rooms, made place for a friend or former townsman and his family. In many instances this was done from unselfish motives and in a humane spirit.

A realization of the need for accurate information concerning the Negro migration, and the belief that in an intelligent treatment of the problem lay the welfare of the entire community as well as that of the local Negro group, prompted the attempt at a scientific study of the situation. The primary purpose of the study was to learn the facts, but there was also a hope that the data obtained might lead to the amelioration of certain existing evils and the prevention of threatening ones.

†The Pittsburgh Graded Tax Law has, apparently, not been in operation long enough to produce the results desired by its sponsors.

In order to ascertain as many of the facts as possible concerning housing conditions, rooming and boarding houses, three or four family tenement houses, single family residences, camps, churches and other lodging places were investigated. A comparative study of health and crime among Negroes of Allegheny County before and after the period of the Northern migration was also attempted.

Storerooms in the Hill District Converted into Family Residences and Rooming Houses.

A questionaire concerning kinds of labor in which Negro migrants engaged, and wages paid them both in Pittsburgh and in their native South was prepared; and answers to it from over five hundred individuals were obtained during the months of July and August, 1917. Information relating to housing, rents, health and social conditions was elicited in a similar manner. An effort was made to visit and study every Negro quarter in Pittsburgh. Data was secured from the Negro sections in the Hill District and upper Wylie and Bedford Avenues; the Lawrenceville district, about Penn Avenue, between Thirty-fourth and Twenty-eighth Streets; the Northside Negro quarter around Beaver Avenue and Fulton Street; the East Liberty section in the vicinity of Mignonette and Shakespeare Streets, and the new downtown Negro section on Second Avenue, Ross and Water Streets.

The information thus secured is discussed in the following pages.

TABLE NUMBER I

Time of Residence in Pittsburgh of 505 Negro Migrants Questioned

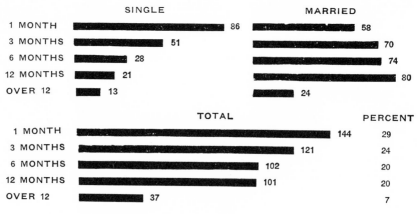

	SINGLE		MARRIED	
1 MONTH	86		58	
3 MONTHS	51		70	
6 MONTHS	28		74	
12 MONTHS	21		80	
OVER 12	13		24	

	TOTAL		PERCENT
1 MONTH	144		29
3 MONTHS	121		24
6 MONTHS	102		20
12 MONTHS	101		20
OVER 12	37		7

  Table No. 1 indicates that the migration has been going on for little longer than one year. Ninety-three percent of those who gave the time of residence in Pittsburgh had been here less than one year. More than eighty percent of the single men interviewed had been here less than six months. In the number who have been here for the longest periods, married men predominate, showing the tendency of this class to become permanent residents. This fact is evidently well known to some industrial concerns which have been bringing men from the South. Many of them have learned from bitter experience that the mere delivery of a train load of men from a Southern city, does not guarantee a sufficient supply of labor. This is evidenced by the fact that the labor agents of some of these firms, made an effort to secure married men only, and even to investigate them prior to their coming here. Differences in recruiting methods may also explain why some employers and labor agents hold a very optimistic view of the Negro as a worker, while others despair of him. The reason why Pittsburgh has been unable to secure a stable labor force is doubtless realized by the local manufacturers. The married Negro comes to the North to stay. He desires to have his family with him, and if he is not accompanied North by his wife and children he plans to have them follow him at the earliest possible date. Although such a man is glad to receive the better treatment, enlarged privileges and higher wages, which are accorded him here, he cannot adjust himself permanently to the Pittsburgh housing situation. He meets his first insuperable difficulty when he attempts to get a house in which to live. Back South, he may have been oppressed, but his home was often in a more comfortable place, where he had light and space. At least he did not have to live in one room in a congested slum and pay excessive rents.

While it is true that the foreign immigrant of a few years ago was probably not accorded any better accommodations in Pittsburgh than is the Negro at present, it should be remembered that the foreigner did not know the language. Everything seemed strange and unfamiliar to him. He was loath to move to an even stranger part of the city and preferred to stay in his first new world home and to live among his own people, even under adverse conditions. It is altogether different with the Negro. He knows the language and the country; he does not fear to migrate and when he does not feel content in one place, he proceeds to look for a better one. We might cite dozens of incidents of men who have either had their families here or intended to bring them, but have gone to other cities where they hoped to find better accommodations. This is certain to continue if cities like Cleveland, Detroit and Philadelphia keep in advance of Pittsburgh in building or providing houses for these migrants. The Pittsburgh manufacturer will never keep an efficient labor supply of Negroes until he learns to compete with the employers of the other cities in a housing programme as well as in wages.

The actual situation of the Pittsburgh housing problem for the Negro is shown by the figures obtained in our survey. Almost ninety-eight percent of the people investigated live either in rooming houses or in tenements containing more than three families. Thirty-five percent live in tenement houses, fifty percent in rooming houses, about twelve percent in camps and churches, and only two and a half percent live in what may be termed single private family residences.

TABLE NUMBER II
Kinds of Residences of 465 Negro Migrants Questioned

	SINGLE	FAMILIES	TOTAL	PERCENT
Tenement	30	133	163	35
Rooming and Boarding	223	9	232	50
One Family House	6	5	11	2.5
Camp	36	0	36	7.5
Mission	23	0	23	5.
	318	147	465	100

11

Of the men without families here, only twenty-two out of more than three hundred had individual bed rooms. Twenty-five percent lived four in a room, and twenty-five percent lived in rooms used by more than four people. Again only thirty-seven percent slept in separate beds, fifty percent slept two in a bed, and thirteen percent sleep three or more in a bed.

TABLE NUMBER III

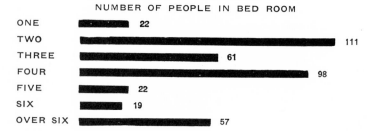

NUMBER OF PEOPLE IN BED ROOM

ONE	22
TWO	111
THREE	61
FOUR	98
FIVE	22
SIX	19
OVER SIX	57

The conditions in these rooming houses often beggar description. Sleeping quarters are provided not only in bedrooms, but also in attics, basements, dining rooms and kitchens. In many instances, houses in which these rooms are located are dilapidated dwellings with the paper torn off, the plaster sagging from the naked lath, the windows broken, the ceiling low and damp, and the whole room dark, stuffy and unsanitary. In one or two instances, these rooms, with more than six people sleeping in them at one time, have practically no openings for either light or air.

A Typical Boarding House on Lower Wylie Avenue.

In the more crowded sections, beds are rented on a double shift basis. Men who work at night sleep during the day in the beds vacated by day workers. There is no space in these rooms, except for beds and as many of them are crowded in as can be possibly accommodated.

There is rarely a place in these rooms for even suitcases or trunks. Under such circumstances the rooms can be kept clean with difficulty, and there is apparently no disposition to wrestle with the dirt and litter. Very few of these sleeping rooms have more than two windows each, and many have only one window. Only a few are provided with bath rooms, while a great number have the water and toilets in the yards or other places outside the house. Many of these roomers complain that often they are not given any soap, and are never given more than one towel a week.

TABLE NUMBER IV
Rents Paid in Rooming Houses by 305 Roomers

		Percentage
168	paid $1.50 per week	55
103	paid $1.75 per week	34
13	paid $2.00 per week	4.25
14	paid $3.00 per week	4.25
7	paid Over $3.00	2.5
		100

The rents paid by these roomers are shown in table number IV. They varied from $1.50 to $3.00 per week, and in a few instances were as high as $4.00 per week. In a number of cases, the men also board in the same place in which they room, paying from five to seven or eight dollars per week for food and shelter.

TABLE NUMBER V.
ONE WEEK'S COST OF BOARD PER MAN

$2 PER WEEK	4
$3 PER WEEK	34
$4 PER WEEK	39
$5 PER WEEK	59
$6 PER WEEK	77
$7 PER WEEK	31
$8 PER WEEK AND OVER	24

The situation in the camps is not better than that in rooming houses. In one railroad camp visited, the men were

13

lodged in box cars, each of which was equipped with four or eight beds, or they were quartered in a row of wooden houses two stories high, each room of which contained from six to eight beds. It is true that the rents charged in this camp were only the nominal sum of five cents per night, or $1.50 per month, but the men had to buy their food from the camp commissary, using company checks, and also had to prepare it themselves. Practically every man interviewed complained of the high prices charged, and that this complaint was not altogether groundless was evident from the scanty purchases being made by these men at the time of the investigator's visit. In another railroad camp, located near Pittsburgh, which was visited in the early spring, about one hundred men were lodged in one big "bunkhouse", containing about fifty double-tier beds. Although there were adequate toilet and shower bath facilities, the beds were unclean. This company also boarded these men, making a flat weekly charge.

Box Cars in a Railroad Camp in Pittsburgh used as Living and Sleeping Quarters.

The rooming houses with one exception are conducted by colored people, who act either as janitors or as hosts. In only one case, as far as our investigation extended, did we find a white woman running a rooming house for colored people. Many of these houses are in reality run by Whites, who keep a colored janitor or manager in the House. Several of the big rooming houses on lower Wylie Avenue, for instance, are conducted for a local white merchant, who keeps a colored janitor in each of them, and only visits them to check the books and collect the rents. In many instances however, houses are operated by colored people, who either run or lease them. Most of these lessees or owners are Pittsburghers, but a few are new-comers, who, having brought a bit of capital with them have opened rooming houses as investments. Some of these people have become the prey of cunning landlords. In one case in the down town section, a colored migrant rented an old and di-lapidated shack, paying fifty dollars a month, and was un-aware that the contract signed by him specified that he pay for his own repairs. The Negro claims that as the house is very old and in such bad condition, it would cost him an ad-ditional fifty dollars each month to keep it habitable.

TABLE NUMBER VI

Number of Rooms Per Family of 157 Negro Families

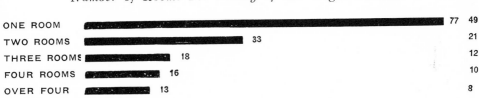

		PERCENT
ONE ROOM	77	49
TWO ROOMS	33	21
THREE ROOMS	18	12
FOUR ROOMS	16	10
OVER FOUR	13	8

The deplorable housing of migrant families is shown in table number VI. Of the 157 families investigated, seventy-seven or 49% live in one room each. Thirty-three or 21% live in two-room apartments, and only forty-seven families or 30% live in apartments of three or more rooms each.

Of these forty-seven families, thirty-eight kept roomers or boarders, totalling one hundred and thirty-one, or an average of 3.5 roomers per family. Eighty-one of the total of one hundred and thirty-nine houses inspected, had water inside the house, while fifty-eight houses secured water from yard or street hydrants or from neighbors. Only thirty-four of the total were equipped with interior toilet facilities; the rest had outside toilets. Of the latter, forty-two had no sewerage con-nections, and used filthy, unsanitary vaults.

The rents paid for the "residences" described above ap-pear in the following table:

Rents Paid by 142 Families Investigated

$10 PER MONTH	41
$15 PER MONTH	60
$20 PER MONTH	18
$25 PER MONTH	13
OVER $25	10

The sections formerly designated as Negro quarters, have been long since congested beyond capacity by the influx of newcomers, and a score of new colonies have sprung up in hollows and ravines, on hill slopes and along river banks, by railroad tracks and in mill-yards. In many instances the dwellings are those which have been abandoned by foreign white people since the beginning of the present war. In some cases they are structures once condemned by the City Bureau of Sanitation, but opened again only to accommodate the influx

A Row of Houses Unused for Several Years Until the Present Influx from the South.

from the South. Very few of these houses are equipped with gas. Coal and wood are used both for cooking and heating. During the hot days of July, the visitor found in several instances a red hot stove in a room which was being used as kitchen, dining room, parlor and bedroom. This, however, did not seem to bother the newcomers, as many of the women, being unaccustomed to the use of gas, and fearful of it, preferred the more accustomed method of cooking.

A few of these families were found living in so-called "basements", more than three-fourths under ground, a direct violation of a municipal ordinance.‡ Some rooms had no other opening than a door. The rents paid for such quarters are often beyond belief. In one of these rooms in the Hill District, where only the upper halves of the windows were level with the sidewalk, lived a man, his wife and their five children, the eldest of whom was sixteen years old. The rental was six dollars per week. Another family paid twenty-five dollars per month for three small rooms on the ground floor. The kitchen was so damp and close that the investigator found it impossible to remain for long, because it was difficult to breathe. The ceilings in many of the houses visited were very low, hardly highe than six or seven feet and the rooms were often piled high with furniture. That the owners of these houses cared little about improving their houses was indicated in several cases by the fact that water faucets and toilets had been out of commission for months, and no effort at repair had been made.

"Basement" Occupied by a Migrant Family. The Only Opening in this Dwelling Appears in the Picture.

Because of these bad conditions many peculiar maladjustments exist. A certain man lived in a rooming house, while his young wife and baby lived in another place. In addition to his own rent and board, he paid ten dollars a week for the keep of his wife and baby. In another case, a family was forced to pay six dollars a month storage on the furniture which they had brought from the South, because their new quarters were too cramped to accommodate it.

‡Pittsburgh Sanitary Code of 1913, Sections 132, 133 and 134, pages 75, 76 and 77.

A goodly number of the migrants have evidently been accustomed to much better living conditions than are offered them here, and in spite of almost insurmountable obstacles, still preserve something of their cleanly habits. Few of these people intend to remain here unless they can get a better place to stay. All complained, some with tears in their eyes, of the bad housing accorded them. As one intelligent and hard working woman who lived in one room expressed it while packing her trunks to go back to Sylvester, Georgia, "I never lived in such houses in my life. We had four rooms in my home." This woman was earning ten dollars per week and her husband was profitably employed, yet they choose to relinquish the comparatively large rewards of the North, rather than do without the decencies of life which they had known in the South.

TABLE NUMBER VIII
Ages of the 506 Migrants Interviewed

	SINGLE	MARRIED	TOTAL	PERCENTAGE
Under 18 years	13	1	14	3
From 18 to 25	115	39	154	30
From 25 to 30	31	63	94	19
From 30 to 40	34	101	135	27
From 40 to 50	7	66	73	14
From 50 to 60	4	28	32	6
60 and over	2	2	4	1
	206	300	506	100

AGES OF MIGRANTS

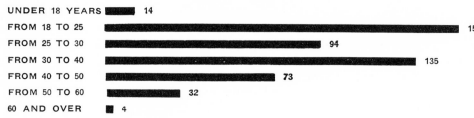

UNDER 18 YEARS   14
FROM 18 TO 25   154
FROM 25 TO 30   94
FROM 30 TO 40   135
FROM 40 TO 50   73
FROM 50 TO 60   32
60 AND OVER   4

Table number VIII is significant because it enables us to shed light upon one important phase of the migration. It appears that more than seventy-five percent of the Southern migrants are between the ages of eighteen and forty. Only ten percent of the 506 people questioned were under eighteen or past fifty years of age. This fact is significant, both to the industrial concerns which are in need of a labor supply and to the community as a whole. For the industrial concerns, it means that these migrants are the most desirable laborers, men at the height of their wealth producing capacity. They satisfy the pressing need which has confronted the local manufacturers since the foreign supply of labor was cut off by the war. From the standpoint of the community, it is important to know that the influx lays few immediate burdens upon the city. There are few minors to be educated and few aged or dependent ones likely to become a public charge.

The percentage of single people between the ages of eighteen and thirty is far greater than that of the married ones, which is a natural expectation. Of the five hundred and thirty persons interviewed, two hundred and nineteen or forty-one and one-half percent were single; one hundred sixty-two or thirty and one-half percent were married, and had already brought their families here, while one hundred and thirty-nine or twenty-eight percent were married, but were here without their families. Ninety-eight of the families had children; thirty-nine of the families had no children here, and seventeen families either had some or all of the children in the South, while the remaining six placed their children under the care of relatives or institutions. The number of children per family of those who had their wives here, varied from one to ten. Forty families had one child each; twenty-three, two children each, fifteen had three children each, and twenty had four or more children each. Nineteen families had one or more children under twenty helping to support them, but only four had more than one child assisting in the support of the family. Among the one hundred and forty-nine persons whose families remained in the South, ninety-six had children and seventeen had none. Of the remainder a number stated that they had one or two of their children with them, while others gave no definite information. Sixty-three of those who had children at home had no more than two children each, while thirty-three had three or more children at home. These figures seem to indicate that the migration is largely that of small families.

The Negro migration from the South into Pittsburgh, while it has been accentuated and accelerated by the present war, which created a greater need for labor, is not in reality an altogether new thing for Pittsburgh. There has been a steady influx of Negroes, though in small numbers, since the pre Civil War days. Pittsburgh and Allegheny were important stations of the Underground Railway, and many a Negro came to Pittsburgh from the near-by slave states, as to a city of refuge. The Negro population in Allegheny County grew

19

steadily from 3431 in 1850 to 34,217 in 1910. The percentage of Negroes in the total population of the County has continually increased within the last four decades. (Two and two-tenths percent in 1880 and three and four-tenths in 1910). Negroes have always been attracted by the opportunities which this city with its abundance of work and good wages could offer them in improving their economic status.

The recent unprecedented influx of Negroes had made the Negro population in Pittsburgh increase more than twice as fast within the last two years as during the entire ten years preceding. The percentage of Negroes in our total population has leaped very suddenly. This fact is sufficient to warrant our serious study and active efforts toward the social orientation and adjustment of the new element in our midst.

Wooden Shacks Used as Living and Sleeping Quarters in a Railroad Camp.

From the standpoint of Pittsburgh's industrial and business interests, however, the migration into this district, has not been at all satisfactory. Pittsburgh as the steel center of the country, is naturally playing a more important part than ever in the present crisis, and has felt a proportionate increase in the need for a labor supply. The Negro migration in Pittsburgh, it can be safely stated, has not usurped the place of the white worker. Every man is needed, as there are more jobs than men to fill them. Pittsburgh's industrial life is for the time being dependent upon the Negro labor supply.

In spite of its necessity, Pittsburgh has not received a sufficient supply of Negroes, and certainly not in the same full proportion as did many smaller industrial towns. Pittsburgh manufacturers are still in need of labor, and this in spite of the fact that the railroads and a few of the industrial concerns of the locality have had labor agents in the South. These agents, laboring under great difficulties because of the obstructive tactics adopted in certain southern communities to prevent the Negro exodus, have nevertheless succeeded in bringing several thousand colored workers into this district. That they have had little success in keeping these people here, is acknowledged by all of them. One company for instance, which imported about a thousand men within the past year, had only about three hundred of these working at the time of the investigator's visit in July, 1917. One railroad, which is said to have brought about fourteen thousand people to the North within the last twelve months, has been able to keep an average of only eighteen hundred at work.

It must be admitted that the labor agents, because of their eagerness to secure as many men as possible, are not particular as to the character of those they are bringing here, and there is therefore a goodly number of idle and shiftless Negroes who are floating and undependable. On the other hand we must not fail to recognize that most migrants come through their own volition, pay their own fares, leave their native states, and break up family connections, because they are in search of better opportunities, social and economic. As a class they appear to be industrious, ambitious, pious and temperate, and are eager to get established with their families.

In the foregoing pages, we have discussed the housing and rooming situation which confronts the Negro. An examination of the kind and hours of work and wages received, discloses another reason why many of these people do not remain here.

TABLE NUMBER IX

*Occupations of Migrants in Pittsburgh as Compared with Statements of Occupations in South**

OCCUPATIONS	IN PITTSBURGH	PER CENTAGE	IN SOUTH	PER CENTAGE
Common Laborer	468	95	286	54
Skilled or semi-skilled	20	4	59	11
Farmer			81	15
Miner			36	7
Saw Mill Workers			9	2
Ran own farm or father's farm			33	6
Ran farm on crop sharing basis			22	5
Other Occupations	5	1	0	0
	493	100	529	100

***The differences in the totals in this table as well as in a few others, are due to the fact that many have given answers to one question and not to the other.

From the foregoing table, it is apparent that ninety-five percent of the migrants who stated their occupations, were doing unskilled labor, in the steel mills, the building trades, on the railroads, or acting as servants, porters, janitors, cooks and cleaners. Only twenty or four percent out of four hundred and ninety-three migrants whose occupations were ascertained, were doing what may be called semi-skilled or skilled work, as puddlers, mold-setters, painters and carpenters. On the other hand, in the South fifty-nine of five hundred and twenty-nine claimed to have been engaged in skilled labor, while a large number were rural workers.

TABLE NUMBER X

Comparison Between Hours of Work Per Day in Pittsburgh and in South

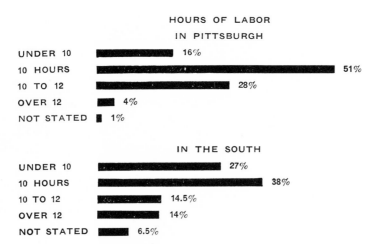

A comparison between work hours of migrants in the South and in Pittsburgh, reveals another interesting feature. As against the twenty-seven percent who were working less than ten hours a day at home, only sixteen percent are working for a like period here. A greater number work a ten-hour day here than in the South, (fifty-one percent as against thirty-eight percent), and there seems to be a greater number working over twelve hours per day before coming North, than afterward. This is probably due to the fact that a considerable body of these men were farm laborers.

22

TABLE NUMBER XI

Comparison of Wages Received Per Day in Pittsburgh and in South

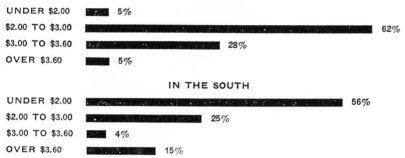

IN PITTSBURGH

UNDER $2.00   5%

$2.00 TO $3.00   62%

$3.00 TO $3.60   28%

OVER $3.60   5%

IN THE SOUTH

UNDER $2.00   56%

$2.00 TO $3.00   25%

$3.00 TO $3.60   4%

OVER $3.60   15%

As to the comparative wages paid here and in the South, it appears from table number X, that the great mass of workers get higher wages here than in the places from which they come, fifty-six percent received less than two dollars a day in the South, while only five percent received such wages in Pittsburgh. However the number of those who said they received high wages in the South is greater than the number of those receiving them here. Fifteen percent said they received more than three dollars and sixty cents a day at home, while only five percent received more than that rate for twelve hours work here. Sixty-seven percent of the four hundred and fifty-three persons stating their earnings here, earn less than three dollars per day. Twenty-eight percent earn from three dollars to three sixty per day, while only five percent earn more than three dollars and sixty cents per day. The average working day for both Pittsburgh and the South is ten and four-tenths hours. The average wage is $2.85 here; in the South it amounted to $2.15. It may be interesting to point out that the number of married men who work longer hours and receive more money is proportionately greater than that of the single men, who have not "given hostages to fortune."

It has been stated frequently that the Negro exodus from the South is in a large measure due to the fact that the Southern states have adopted prohibition. While it is true that most of the newcomers are from prohibition states, our figures, however, do not warrant the conclusion that the Negroes came North to use the saloon. We are inclined to believe that the answers to this question were sincere. The classification of "drinkers" includes all persons who imbibe however infrequently and those who drink beer only. Out of the four hundred and seventy-seven persons who answered these questions, two hundred and ten or forty-four percent said that they drank, while two hundred and sixty-seven or fifty-six percent were total abstainers. It is interesting to note that among those who have families in Pittsburgh, the percentage of those who drink is smaller than among those who are single or have families elsewhere. Thirty percent of the former class drink, while seventy percent do not drink at all. The percentage of drinkers of those with their families at home, is even greater than those of the single people, which may be explained by the fact that many of the younger people have as yet not acquired the drink habit.

The church going proclivity of the Negro is well known and is borne out by our study. Of the four hundred and eighty-nine who replied to this question, three hundred and seventy or almost seventy-six percent are either church members or attendants, and only one hundred and nineteen or twenty-four percent do not attend any church.

Proof that these newcomers are not all lazy, shiftless, and immoral is to be found in the statements of savings, and of remittances to relatives in the South. Fifteen percent of the families here had savings. Eighty percent§ of the married ones with families elsewhere were sending money home, and nearly one hundred of the two hundred and nineteen single people interviewed, were contributing sums to parents, sisters or other relatives. Most of these contributions, (sixty-five percent) amounted to about five dollars per week. Fifty-two persons were contributing from five to ten dollars per week, and seven were sending over ten dollars per week.

From table number XII, it seems that only a few of the Southern states have borne the brunt of the exodus. Alabama, Georgia, North Carolina and Virginia taken together, have contributed sixty percent of the migrants, Alabama and Georgia giving forty-seven percent of the total number. Alabama was the native state of more than forty-nine percent of the married men who have families here. This altogether disproportionate influx from Alabama, as compared with other states, is probably due to the fact that our state and the former have similar industries. Birmingham, Alabama, as is well known, is called the "Pittsburgh of the South"; and it is therefore natural that

§The cause for many of these migrants not contributing to the support of their families may be explained by the fact that they have not been here long enough to get established.

24

the labor agents from this district should make a special effort to secure the labor which is more or less familiar with the iron and steel business. Again, it may be presumed that a great many who were working in the steel industries or in the mines of Alabama have come to Pittsburgh in order to secure familiar employment. A considerable number, however, may have come because of the crop failure and the ravages of the boll-weevil which have made the cultivation of cotton unprofitable during recent years.

TABLE NUMBER XII

Home States of 567 Migrants

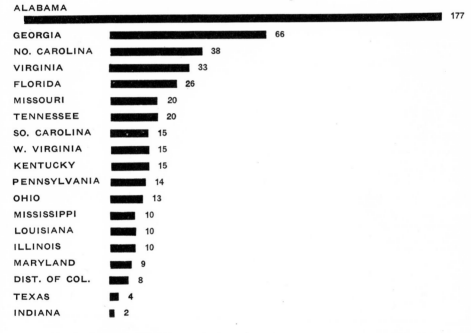

ALABAMA	177
GEORGIA	66
NO. CAROLINA	38
VIRGINIA	33
FLORIDA	26
MISSOURI	20
TENNESSEE	20
SO. CAROLINA	15
W. VIRGINIA	15
KENTUCKY	15
PENNSYLVANIA	14
OHIO	13
MISSISSIPPI	10
LOUISIANA	10
ILLINOIS	10
MARYLAND	9
DIST. OF COL.	8
TEXAS	4
INDIANA	2

Undoubtedly many Negroes have come to the North in response to the seductive arts of labor agents, who worked on a per capita commission basis. These emissaries, both in the North and in the South, made glowing promises of high wages, social equality, and better living conditions above the Mason-Dixon Line. But these inducements were probably not the underlying factor of the migration. They merely gave opportunity for the expression of a growing discontent engendered by many years of oppression. Segregation, lynchings, economic exploitation, and the denial of educational freedom, justice and constitutional right, had filled the Negro's cup of bitterness to overflowing. The South was to his mind still a place of bondage for him and in the North he saw that long dreamed Land of Promise where he might live more freely.

Three hundred and ninety-five of the four hundred and seventy-four when questioned as to who paid their transportation North replied that they paid their own fare, while only seventy-nine admitted they were brought here at the expense of railroads and other industrial concerns. Numerous stories of persecutions by the White South on trumped up charges of all sorts are told by these migrants. Many of them say they had to leave their homes in secrecy and at night, and to walk

Typical Dwellings of Negro Migrants.

to some station where they were not known, before they could board a train for the North. Many reported that they were unable to secure tickets at home, and had to secure them from the North. If tickets were discovered in the possession of a Negro, they were confiscated and destroyed by the police. At times when three or more Negroes were found together, they were suspected of "conspiring to go North"; some mythical charge was brought against them, and they were arrested. Threats and intimidation of all kinds were used against these migrants, both at home and on the train. One very intelligent Negro of about forty who owned property in Alabama related some of the persecutions which he had borne while at home. He told of taking the train at night several miles away from his own

26

town, and of being accosted on board by a white Southerner who pointed to the next car which contained several coffins and said, "Yo Niggahs goin' to Pittsburgh, eh? We all are jes shippin' five of yo back from thah. They froze to death in Pittsburgh." It may be interesting to remark that this occured in June, 1917, when Pittsburgh was sweltering in the heat of early summer.

Of the more than four hundred men who stated their reasons for coming North, three hundred and twenty-five said that the higher wages and economic opportunities here had attracted them. Two hundred and eighty-eight of these also included better treatment as one of the factors in their migration. As one of them expressed it, "If I were half as well treated home as here, I would rather stay there, as I had my family there and had a better home and better health." Eighty-five had no special reason for their coming, and were "jes travelin' to see the country", or the like. Twenty-five were either tired of their work or wanted to change it. This was the case particularly with the miners from West Virginia and Alabama. Twenty-seven had either lost their jobs, were out of work, or had various other reasons for coming. These figures seem to indicate that the prime causes of the migration are rather fundamental, and not merely temporary.

The Negro migration is similar to the previous European immigration because, while dominantly economic, it is also due to social and political maladjustments; but it is more largely a family migration. For the number of Negroes who brought women and children with them is greater in proportion to the total than was the case with the foreigners. The European usually came alone and sent for his family after a considerable lapse of time. The Negro either brings his family with him or sends for it within the first three or four months following his arrival. The complication of our housing problem is obvious under these circumstances, for Pittsburgh until the present time has attempted to meet the housing requirements of only single men workers of the new labor group.

The short-sightedness of our failure to provide decent homes in the city, in order to retain the labor which is so essential for the expansion of Pittsburgh and the growth of its industries, is again exposed by the figures in our study. Of the three hundred and thirty single men, or men without families here, answering the question as to whether they will remain here, return South or move elsewhere, only ninety-two or twenty-eight percent said they would remain here. A hundred and thirty-seven or forty-two percent were going back or somewhere else, while one hundred and one or thirty percent were still undecided.

As for the reasons why these men would not remain in the city, seventy-nine or fifty-seven percent were leaving because they could not get a better room because the rents paid by them were too excessive for the wages received; thirty-seven or twenty-seven percent, gave family connections as their reason, and the remaining sixteen percent either had no reasons or were leaving because of ill health, bad climate or other unfavorable conditions. The difficulty of securing an adequate labor supply for Pittsburgh is thus, in part, explained by the very nature of the economic problems involved.

CHAPTER II.

THE NEGRO'S OWN PROBLEM

The Negro migration is neither an isolated nor a temporary phenomenon, but the logical result of a long series of linked causes beginning with the landing of the first slave ship and extending to the present day. The slavery which was ended by the Emancipation Proclamation and the Fourteenth Amendment of the National Constitution has been succeeded by less sinister, but still significant social and economic problems, which are full of subtle menace for the welfare of America.

The intelligent Negro has long believed that his only escape from the measure of suppression which still exists is to go to the North, and he has seized the opportunity whenever it was presented to him. The present unprecedented influx of black workers from the South is merely the result of a sudden expansion of opportunity due to a war-depleted labor market in the North. The causes for his migration are basically inherent in the social and economic system which has kept him down for these long years in the South. The Negro is beginning to appreciate his own value and duties, and is proceeding to the North where he knows he can at least enjoy a measure of justice. This naturally means a tremendous problem for the North. The race question is no longer confined to the states below the Mason and Dixon Line, but becomes the concern of the whole nation. It may be presumed that the European immigration after this war will not be as great as it was before it.

28

The Negro is taking the place of the foreign worker, and he is certain to become an increasingly important factor in our national political and industrial life. He is already an important political factor in some municipalities; he is soon to be a basic factor in our industries. The Negro who has lived in the North has taken advantage of the industrial opportunities which were open to him, and is continuing to do so more and more.

Our policy of *laissez-faire* adopted towards the European immigrant can no longer be contained. This war has taught us some great lessons, and probably the greatest of all is the lesson of the necessity for a redefinition of social terms, and a reconsideration of human values. It has made us realize that if we want the nation to stand united in times of stress our policy must be consistent at all times. Democracy we have learned in this struggle, no longer means "each for himself, and the devil take the hind-most." If it means anything at all, it is that we are "members one of another", and that an injury to one is an injury to and the concern of all. Our old policy has shown us that the devil has taken too many, and we have come to say, "Halt!" This must no longer continue. We must see that all the elements which go to make up our body-politic are adjusted and placed in their proper relation. Our traditional attitude, this struggle has taught us, is too costly and we cannot afford longer to continue it. We know now that it is not sufficient that a few may have democracy and freedom while the rest are denied economic opportunity. We are also coming to realize that "we cannot hold a part of our fellow-men down in the gutter without remaining there ourselves."

No exact estimate of the number of Negroes who have come North within the last year is possible. Estimates vary from three hundred thousand to seven hundred thousand. There are probably about two million Negroes now living in the North, and it is of paramount importance that we look into the conditions of these people who although in our midst, are yet so little known to us, and see that they are fitted into their new environment. Our little study of the social opportunities available, and the conditions existing among our Negro brethren may therefore be of great interest, and we are glad to present here some of the facts which were disclosed in our survey of these people who have recently settled amongst us, in order to avail themselves of our hospitality, and industrial opportunities. We have discussed in the preceding pages the immediate opportunities for Negroes in this city as to housing and wages. It may therefore not be amiss to discuss the possibilities of his attaining an advanced political, social and economic status.

Politically, the Negro in Pittsburgh is as free as the whites of the same group. Coming from places where the vote is denied him, he is naturally very glad to receive the privilege in Pittsburgh. It is a well known fact that the Negro vote is often a deciding factor in the results of municipal elections. Although there are a few shrewd Negro politicians, and the Negro vote is frequently *"en bloc"* there is never an issue made on some particular Negro problem. All candidates seem to assume that there is no special issue that concerns the Negro more than any other group in the city, and unscrupulous Negro politicians are not in the least perturbed. They always see to it, however, that no Negro vote will be lost, that their occupation tax is paid, and that they are registered. This was clearly brought out in this year's municipal election. Although the Negro vote was a great factor in deciding this campaign, not one of the candidates made an issue of the housing and other problems which are confronting the Negroes at present. It can therefore be stated that in politics, while the Negro has been utilized by all sorts of politicians, he has at least nominally been as free as his white brother in the same position.

However, more and more we are coming to realize that political freedom without industrial opportunities means but little. Democracy must also mean industrial opportunity, and social democracy, as well as political democracy. But the industrial opportunity which the Negro demands is not even the same as is demanded by his more fortunate white-skinned brother. While his fellow-human beings demand a larger voice in industry and business, and a greater share of the product, the Negro is still meekly begging for his inalienable right to participate in industry, to help extend and build it up. It is the denial of this right that confronts the Negro in the North. and makes his problem of paramount significance.

The great majority of the Negro migrants come North because of the better economic and social opportunities here. But even here they are not permitted to enter industry freely. They are kept in the ranks of unskilled labor and in the field of personal service. Until the present demand for unskilled labor arose, the Negroes in the North were for the most part, servants. There were very few Negroes occupied otherwise than

30

as porters, chauffeurs, janitors and the like. The **Negro at** present has entered the productive industries, but he is kept still on the lowest rung of the economic ladder.

TABLE NUMBER XIII

List of Industrial Concerns Visited in the Pittsburgh District

NAME OF CONCERN	No. of Negroes employed at present.	No. employed prior to 1916.	% doing un-skilled labor.	Wages per hour of un-skilled labor.	No. of hours per day.
Carnegie Steel Co. (all plants)	4,000	1,500	95%	30c	8 to 12
Jones & Laughlin	1,500	400	100%	30c	10
Westinghouse Elec. & Mfg. Co.	900	25	90%	28-30c	10
Harbison & Walker	250	50	80%	27½c	10
National Tube Co. (all plants)	250	100	100%	30c	10
Pressed Steel Car Co.	25	25	50%	23c	11
Pgh. Forge & Iron	75	0	100%	30c	10
Moorhead Brothers	200	200	75%	30c	10
Am. Steel & Wire	25	25	100%	28-30c	10
Clinton Iron & Steel	25	25	75%		
Oliver Iron & Steel	50	0	100%	25-28c	10
Carbon Steel Co.	200	50	75%	30c	10-12
Crucible Steel Co.	400	150	90%	28-33c	10
A. M. Byers Co.	200	0	60%		10
Lockhart Steel Co.	160	0	95%	27½c	10
Mesta Machine Co.	50	0	100%	30c	10
Marshall Foundry Co.	15	0			
U. S. Glass Co.			No Negroes employed		
Thompson-Sterret Co.			No Negroes employed		
Spang-Chalfant Co.			No Negroes employed		
	8,325	2,550			

From a study of colored employees in twenty of the largest industrial plants, in the Pittsburgh district, arbitrarily select-ed (Table No. XIII), we find that most of the concerns have employed colored labor only since May or June of 1916. Very

*The figures in this table were secured during the months of July and August 1917, and have probably been changed since.

few of the Pittsburgh industries have used colored labor in capacities other than as janitors and window cleaners. A few of the plants visited had not begun to employ colored people until in the spring of 1917, while a few others had not yet come to employ Negroes, either because they believed the Negro workers to be inferior and inefficient, or because they feared that their white labor force would refuse to work with the blacks. The Superintendent of one big steel plant which has not employed colored labor during the past few years admitted that he faced a decided shortage of labor, and that he was in need of men; but he said he would employ Negroes only as a last resort, and that the situation was as yet not sufficiently acute to warrant their employment. In a big glass plant, the company attempted to use Negro labor last winter, but the white workers "ran them out" by swearing at them, calling them "Nigger" and making conditions so unpleasant for them that they were forced to quit. This company has therefore given up any further attempts at employing colored labor. It may be interesting to note, however, that one young Negro boy who pays no attention to such persecution persistently stays there.

About ninety-five percent of the colored workers in the steel mills visited in our survey were doing unskilled labor. In the bigger plants, where many hundreds of Negroes are employed, almost one hundred percent are doing common labor, while in the smaller plants, a few might be found doing labor which required some skill. The reasons alleged by the manufacturers are; first, that the migrants are inefficient and unstable, and second, that the opposition to them on the part of white labor prohibits their use on skilled jobs. The latter objection is illustrated by the case of the white bargemen of a big steel company who wanted to walk out because black workers were introduced among them, and who were only appeased by the provision of separate quarters for the Negroes. While there is an undeniable hostility to Negroes on the part of a few white workers, the objection is frequently exaggerated by prejudiced gang bosses.

That this idea is often due to the prejudice of the heads of departments and other labor employers, was the opinion of a sympathetic superintendent of one of the largest steel plants, who said that in many instances it was the superintendents and managers themselves, who are not alive to their own advantage and so oppose the Negro's doing the better classes of work. The same superintendent said that he had employed Negroes for many years; that a number of them have been connected with his company for several years; that they are just as efficient as the white people. More than half of the twenty-five Negroes in his plant were doing semi-skilled and even skilled work. He had one or two colored foremen over colored gangs, and cited an instance of a colored man drawing a hundred and fourteen dollars in his last two weeks pay. This claim was supported by a very intelligent Negro who was stopped a few blocks away from the plant and questioned as to the conditions in the plant. While admitting everything that the Superintendent said, and stating that there is now absolute free opportunity for colored people in that plant, the man claimed that these conditions have come into being only within the last year. The same superintendent told of an episode illustrating the amicable relations existing in his shop between the white and black workers. He related that a gang of workers had come to him with certain complaints and the threat of a walk-out. When their grievances had been satisfactorily adjusted, they pointed to the lonely black man in their group and said that they were not ready to go back unless their Negro fellow worker was satisfied.

The Migration in Process.

From our survey of the situation it must be evident that the southern migrants are not as well established in the Pittsburgh industries as is the white laborer. They are as yet unadapted to the heavy and pace-set labor in our steel mills. Accustomed to the comparatively easy-going plantation and farm work of the South, it will take some time until these migrants

33

have found themselves. The roar and clangor of our mills make these newcomers a little dazed and confused at first. They do not stay long in one place, being birds of passage; they are continually searching for better wages and accommodations. They cannot even be persuaded to wait until pay day, and they like to get money in advance, following the habit they have acquired from the southern economic system. It is often secured on very flimsy pretexts and spent immediately in the saloons and similar places. It is admitted, however, by all employers of labor, that the Negro who was born in the North or has been in the North for some time, although not as subservient to bad treatment, is as efficient as the white; that because of his knowledge of the language and the ways of this country, he is often much better than the foreign laborer who understands neither.

Paradoxical as it may seem, the labor movement in America—which it is claimed was begun and organized primarily to improve the conditions of all workers, and protect their interests from the designs of heartless and cruel industrial captains—has not only made no effort to relieve and help the oppressed black workers who have suffered even more than the whites from exploitation and serfdom, but in many instances have remained indifferent to the economic interests and even served as an obstacle to the free development of the colored people.

Since the East St. Louis race riots in July of this year, and later on the Chester and other race clashes, the press has been full of controversy concerning the colored labor problem in the North. Employers as well as many prominent persons openly laid the blame for the spilling of the blood of women and little children at the door of the labor unions. On the other hand, the labor men almost as a unit have charged the responsibility for these riots to the Northern industrial leaders who are bringing these laborers to be used as a tool to break up the labor movement in the North.

The motives of the employers who are bringing the colored migrants are obviously not altruistic. They are not concerned primarily with freeing the Negro from the economic and political restrictions to which he is still subjected in the South. It is not to be assumed that their interests extend further than the employment of these ignorant people as unskilled laborers. Indeed the sheer economic interest of the Northern industrial concerns which are bringing the Negro migrants, may be illustrated by the following contract, which is typical of many agreements signed by migrants when accepting transportation North.

"It is hereby understood that I am to work for the above named Company as..................................., the rate of pay to be.................................. The .... Railroad agrees to furnish transportation and food to destination. I agree to work on any part of the .... Railroad where I may be assigned. I further agree to reimburse the .... Railroad for the cost of my railroad transportation, in addition to which I agree to pay ....to cover the cost of meals and other expenses incidental to my employment.

I authorize the Company to deduct from my wages money to pay for the above expenses.

In consideration of the .... Railroad paying my carfare, board, and other expenses, I agree to remain in the service of the aforesaid Company until such time as I reimburse them for the expenses of my transportation, food, etc.

It is agreed upon the part of the Railroad Company that if I shall remain in the service for one year, the .... Railroad Company agrees to return to me the amount of carfare from point of shipment to.......................... By continuous service for one year is meant that I shall not absent myself from duty any time during the period without the consent of my superior officer.

It is understood by me that the .... Railroad will not grant me free transportation to the point where I wa employed.

I am not less than twenty-one or more than forty-five years of age, and have no venereal disease. If my statement in this respect is found to be incorrect this contract becomes void."

....
Laborer's Name.

It is apparent that since the war has put a stop to the importation of foreign immigrants, the Negroes are so far the only cheap and unorganized labor supply obtainable. Indeed Mexicans were brought to work here in the same way, although the experience with them was not as satisfactory as with the blacks.

While it may be true that the motive for bringing these ignorant workers is primarily to fill up the unskilled labor gap, and not to break up the labor movement, it is self-evident that the employers would scarcely admit the latter motive even

35

though it was paramount. It may be, that ultimately the employers may use these workers against the union organizations or against the securing of the eight-hour-day, which the local unions are aiming to attain. Indeed, the employment agent of one of our great industrial plants, which underwent a big strike a few years ago, pointed out that one of the great values of the Negro migration lies in the fact that it gives him a chance to "mix up his labor forces and to establish a balance of power", as the Negro, he claimed, "is more individualistic, does not like to group and does not follow a leader, as readily as some foreigners do." However, in only one instance in our survey of the Pittsburgh Trade Unions, was a complaint lodged against colored people taking the places of striking white workers. This was in a waiters' strike and was won just the same, because the patrons of the restaurants protested against the substitution of Negro waiters. In all the others, there were no such occurrences. Indeed, the number of Negroes taking the places of striking whites and of skilled white workers is so small that it is hardly appreciable. They are, as we have seen, largely taking the places which were left vacant by the unskilled foreign laborers since the beginning of the war, and the new places created by the present industrial boom. No effective effort has been made to organize these unskilled laborers by the recognized American labor movement. These people, therefore, whose places are now being taken by the Negroes, worked under no American standard of labor, and the fear of these unskilled laborers breaking down labor standards which have never existed, is obviously unfounded.

The generalization cannot also be made that the colored people are difficult to organize, for from our survey we have found only one Union, the Waiter's Local, that has made any attempt to organize the colored people, and was unsuccessful. The official of this Union explains it because the colored waiters "are more timid, listen to their bosses, and also have a kind of distrust of the white Unions." The same official also admitted that while he himself would have no objection to working with colored people, the rank and file of his Union would not work on the same floor with a colored waiter. None of the other Unions made any effort to organize the colored workers in their respective trades, and they cannot therefore complain of the difficulty of organizing the Negroes.

In the two trade organizations which admit Negroes to membership, the colored man has proved to be as good a unionist as his white fellows. A single local of the Hod Carriers

Union, a strong labor organization, has over four hundred Negroes among its six hundred members, and has proved how easy it is to organize even the new migrants by enlisting over one hundred and fifty southern hod carriers within the past year.

The other Union which admits Negroes—The Hoisting Engineers' Union, has a number of colored people in its ranks. Several of these are charter-members, and a number have been connected with the organization for a considerable time. Judging from the strength of these Unions—the only ones in the city which have a considerable number of blacks amongst them —the Negroes have proved as good Union men as the whites. If the Pittsburgh trade organizations are typical of the present national trade union movement it would appear that there is little hope for the Negroes. If the present policy of the American labor movement continues, the Negroes can depend but little upon this great liberating force for their advancement. A few facts disclosed in our canvas of the trade unions in Pittsburgh will bear out our statements.

A Row of Dilapidated Old Dwellings in the Downtown Section Used as Rooming Houses for Migrants.

An official of a very powerful Union which has a membership of nearly five thousand said that it had about five colored members. He admitted that there are several hundred Negroes working in the same trade in this city, but his organization does not encourage them to organize and will admit one of them only when he can prove his ability in his work— a technical excuse for exclusion. This official was a man who was born in the South; he believed in the inferiority of the Negro, deplored the absence of a Jim Crow system, and was greatly prejudiced.

Another official of an even more powerful trade union was greatly astonished when he learned that there are white people who take an interest in the Negro question. He absolutely refused to give any information and did not think it was worth while to answer such questions, although he admitted that his union had no colored people and would never accept them. There are, however, several hundred Negroes working at this trade in the city. White members related numerous incidents of white unionists leaving a job when a colored man appeared. Several other unions visited had no Negroes in the union although there were some local colored people in their respective trades.

The typical attitude of the complacent trade unionist is illustrated by a letter which was written by a very prominent local labor leader, a member of the "Alliance for Labor and Democracy" in answer to certain questions asked him. This official refused to state anything orally, and asked that the questions be put to him in writing. His answers, we may presume, have been carefully worded after considerable contemplation of the problem.

The letter begins: "While I do not wish to appear evasive, I do not think some of the questions should have been asked me at this time." Questions and answers follow:

Q. Number of white members in the Union?

A. Our Union has had a growth of one hundred percent in the past six months in the Pittsburgh district.

Q. Number of colored people in the Union?

A. None.

Q. Has there been an increase in the colored labor in your trade within the last year? If so, state approximately the proportion.

A. Yes, estimates can be made only by the employer, as we do not control all shops.

Q. Has there been an increase in the colored union membership within the last year or two?

A. Yes, statistics can be gotten from Mr. Frank Morrison, Secretary, American Federation of Labor, Washington, D. C.

Q. What efforts does your Union make to organize the colored people in your trade?

38

A. Same effort as all others, as the A. F. of L. does not bar any worker on account of race or creed.

Q. Has any colored person applied for membership in your Union within the last year?

A. Yes.

Q. Have the colored people in your trade asked for a separate charter?

A. Not that I know of.

Q. Do you personally know of any complaint by a person of color against your Union as regards race discrimination?

A. Yes.

The official admits that there are colored workers in his trade, that some have applied for membership, and that there have been complaints of race discrimination. His statement concerning efforts to organize Negro laborers would seem to have little meaning in view of his assertion that the growth of white membership during the past year was one hundred percent, while that of Negro membership was zero.

It may, however, be interesting to note that a man who joined this Union about the time this letter was written, said the President of the Union gave him the following pledge:

"I pledge that I will not introduce for membership into this Union anyone but a sober, industrious, WHITE person."

Very often union officials are apt to point to their constitutions which guarantee that no color line be established, and say that the colored people make little effort to organize, and that they are really not trying to get into the Union. "Why don't the Negroes organize locals of their own?" they ask. The assertion that colored people are making little effort to become organized is undoubtedly true, for it may be presumed that if they had continuously, insistently and in sufficient numbers knocked at the doors of the trade unions the barriers would have been unable to withstand the strain and would have opened to them. But unfortunately the attitude of the trade unions developed among the Negroes a feeling of hopelessness which is detrimental to both the Negroes and the labor movement. "What's the use?" is the reply usually given by skilled colored workers when asked why they do not join the unions. They know well enough that they will not be admitted, and that even if they were accepted they could never hope to secure a job from the Union. This spirit goes even further, and is fraught with the most imminent danger. A very intelligent colored labor official said, that there is developing among many Negroes the feeling that the most laudable action is to do anything which will harm or break the labor movement.

That this fatalistic and dangerous attitude of the colored people is not groundless is again evidenced from our study of the situation. The attempt of union officials to becloud or to ignore the issue by saying that the colored people make no effort to become Union members, and do not try to organize their own locals is disclosed by the following case:

A Row of Model Houses Originally Built by a Steel Company for its Colored Workers, but used by Foreign Laborers at Present Because of the Protest of the People in the Neighborhood.

On January 1st, 1917, a group of about thirty unorganized Negro plasterers sent the following letter to the Operative Plasterer's and Cement Finishers' International Association of the United States with offices at Middletown, Ohio.

Pittsburgh, Pa., January 1st, 1917.

"We, the undersigned Colored Plasterers of the City of Pittsburgh, met in a session on the above named date, and after forming an Organization for our mutual benefit voted to petition to you our grievances on the grounds of being discriminated against because of our color. We therefore would like to have a Local Body of our own for our people. We also voted to ask you for the advice and consideration of such a movement, and hereby petition you that you grant us a license for a local of our own, to be operated under your jurisdiction, praying this will meet with your approval, and hoping to get an early reply.

40

This will show that to date we have the support of the men here listed besides a few more. Officers elected so far are as follows:"

The signatures of the officers and twenty-five members follow.

The International then sent the following reply:

"Replying to your letter, we are writing our Pittsburgh Local today in reference to your application for charter. According to the rules and regulations of our organization, no organization can be chartered in any city where we have a Local without consulting the older Organization."

This was signed by the Secretary of the International Association.

The Pittsburgh Local then invited the Secretary of the colored organization to appear at their regular meeting. When the Secretary came, they told him he could have five minutes time in which to present his claims. Nothing resulted from this meeting and no written statement whatsoever was made by the Pittsburgh Local in spite of attempts to secure such.

On a further appeal to the International, the Secretary of the Colored Plasterer's Organization received the following letter from the International Secretary.

"Replying to your letter, I enclose a copy of our constitution and refer you to section No. 34, page No. 8, which means that no charter can be issued to your organization unless approved by No. 31 of Pittsburgh, Pa."

An official of Local number 31 admitted that the rank and file would never consent to have colored people among them, and attend the social functions given by the Union, although he claimed they could not possibly reject a man because of his color, as it is a gross violation of their constitution. He explained the reasons for his local refusing a separate charter to the Negroes as follows: First, that if a charter would be granted to them, they would all become members for the nominal charter fee while their initiation fee for individuals amounts to thirty dollars, and this he said would be a discrimination in favor of the Negroes. But the greatest objection was that the colored plasterers asked for a smaller scale of wages, ($4.50 a day as compared with $6 for whites). When questioned as to his reason why the colored people would not prefer a higher wage, he explained that they could not get work as no one would employ a person of color at the same wages as a white person.*

*The fear that admitting local Negroes to the trade unions would flood the city with skilled Southern Negroes, was given as a reason by one Negro for the exclusion of his race-men from the unions, but was not mentioned by any of the white union officials.

The Secretary of the short-lived colored organization gave as his reason for not joining the Union as an individual the fact that he was aware that the Union, even were he a member, would not supply him with a job, and that white Union men would walk out were he by any chance to be employed.

Another illustration of the difficulty confronting the colored person when he desires to join a Union, is the following: Two colored migrants, J. D. and C. S., painters from Georgia, had applied to the Union for membership in November and December 1916, respectively. Both of these persons have their families here, and claim fourteen and sixteen years' experience in the trade, stating also that they can do as good a job as any other union man. Each one of these claims to have made from $25 to $30 a week in the South by contracting. The official in the office of the Union whom they approached to ask for membership unceremoniously told them that it would take no colored men into membership. The result was that one of these men was fortunate enough to find work in his own line in a non-union shop, receiving twenty dollars per week for eight and one-half hours, as compared with $5.50 for an eight hour day, the union scale. The second man, however, was not so fortunate, and unable to find work in his own line, he is now working as a common laborer in a steel plant making $2.70 for ten hours per day. That many of the colored skilled people do not attempt to join the union because they know the existing situation is obvious. The brother-in-law of one of the above men, also a skilled worker, when asked why he did not try to join the Union, characteristically shrugged his shoulders and uttered the fatalistic "What's the use?"

The following case which throws light on the general situation, and illustrates the resultant effects of this injustice was related by the head clerk of the State Employment Bureau of this city.

"In the month of June, 1917, a man giving the name of P. Bobonis, a Porto Rican, came to our office and asked for work as a carpenter. Mr. Bobonis was a union carpenter, a member of the Colorado State Union. The first place he was sent they told him they were filled up, and when a call was made to determine if the company had sufficient carpenters, the foreman said that it was impossible for them to employ a colored carpenter as all of the white men would walk out, but that they were still badly in need of carpenters. It was then decided to call upon the different companies recognizing the union, to see if they all felt the same way. Much to our amazement we found it to be the general rule—the colored man could pay his initiation fee and dues in the Union, but after that was done he was left little hopes for employment. Four large companies were called for this man and he could not be placed. As a last attempt, a call on the Dravo Contracting Company was made and as they have some union and others non-union men, they employed the man.

Mr. Bobonis was not a floater, but a good man. He is a graduate of Oberlin College and is now working to raise enough money to enable him to study medicine."

Although the attitude of the recognized American Labor movement on the colored question is generally known, the great mass of people are easily misled and appealed to on race lines. It is unfortunate that often a race issue is made of a purely labor question. An episode of the past winter is a case in point. The drivers in one of our department stores had organized themselves into a union and were locked out. The department store immediately substituted colored non-union drivers. Appeals to union people based on race issues were then carried to the patrons of that store until the department store was forced to discharge all of its colored drivers and re-instate the white ones. This was done in spite of the fact that the Union was not recognized, and was broken up, and although the manager of the store is said to have admitted that almost half of the colored drivers had proved one hundred percent efficient.

The difficulties and slow progress made in organizing the laboring classes generally is apparent to anyone who reflects that in spite of the long years of continued effort, and in spite of the fact that in many instances there was no resistance from the employers, hardly ten percent of the working population of the United States is organized in trade and industrial unions today. The problem is difficult for the white men, and it is exceedingly more difficult for the blacks. The white laboring classes have to contend only with the manufacturers. The Negroes, however, have to contend with the white trade unions as well as with the employers.

Until recently, very few colored people in the North were working in trades where the whites were organized. The great mass of Negroes were doing work of the personal service character, and acted as porters, janitors, elevator men, etc. This class of workers is extremely difficult to organize even among the whites. Within the past two years, however, Negroes have in increasing numbers entered the trades which have been organized by the whites. Being refused admission to most of the white unions the only thing the colored man can do is to form his own organization. The first step toward organizing the Negro working man and woman was taken in New York City in July 1917, when the Associated Colored Employees of America was organized. The bulletin used by this organization states that its purpose is to give "facts concerning conditions in the North compiled for the benefit of those who some day expect or desire to be actually free." This organization aims to function as an employment bureau advising members where particular work may be found, and to give general information to those workers who are eager to come from the South.

Rear View of Tenement Near Soho Dump. Note Refuse on Left and Street Level on Right.

The difficulty in organizing the colored people into a separate organization along Trade Union Lines was thus explained by a very prominent Negro leader. The Negro, he said, is escaping from the tyranny of the South to the freedom of the North. In the North he is opposed and at times even mobbed by white laboring men. Strange as it may seem, the industrial captain in the North is the Negro's only friend. He at least is interested in him; he goes after him to bring him North, provides food and shelter for him, pays him better wages than he received in the South, and in many instances gives him medical attention, and helps him bring his family

44

here. Can you expect him under the circumstances to alienate and betray his only friend in the North, for the trade unions whom he fears and distrusts?

It is obvious that the trade unions will have to make a more attractive appeal to convince the Negro that they are really his best friends. Their duty and policy are clear. Theirs is a struggle for the protection of the working people, in order to secure for all the oppressed some of the enjoyments of life. Theirs is a continuous battle for organization, the organization of all workers, irrespective of race, color and creed.

The Negro's own problem and his tragedy in slavery and in freedom is probably best summarized in the following lines taken from the Emporia Gazette and written by William Allen White:

"If the black man loafs in the South he starves. If he works in the South he is poorly paid, more or less in kind—chips and whetstones—and his wife becomes a 'pan-toter.' If he leaves his own estate in the South and goes to work in Northern industry, he is mobbed and killed."

"He was brought to these shores from Africa a captive. He is held by his captors in economic bondage today—forbidden to rise above the lowest serving class. He is herded by himself in a ghetto, and if, while he is there, he reverts to the jungle type, he is burned alive. If he tries to break out of his ghetto, and, by assimilating the white man's civilization, rise, he is driven out by his white brothers."

"If he goes to school, he becomes discontented and is unhappy and dissatisfied with his social status. If he does not go to school and remains ignorant, he is then only a 'coon,' whom everybody exploits, and who has to cheat and swindle in return, or go down in poverty to begging and shame. There aren't ships enough in the world to take him back to the land of his freedom; there isn't enough for him here except on the crowded bottom rung of the ladder, and there, always, the grinding heel of those climbing over him topward is mangling his black hands."

"Race riots, lynchings, political ostracism, social boycott, economic serfdom. No wonder he sings:

"Hard Trials—
"Great tribulations,
"Hard trials—
"I'm gwine for to live with the Lord!"

No wonder as he looks dismally back at the forest whence he came, and dismally forward to the hopeless set to which he is

45

slowly being pushed, he lifts his plaintive voice in its heart-broken minor and wails:

"Swing low, sweet chariot, comin' for to carry me home!"

"*Home*" is about the only place he can go, where they don't oppress him."

THE COMMUNITY'S PROBLEM

CHAPTER III

A Delinquency Study of the Negro in Pittsburgh

An understanding of the conduct and morality of the new comer and stranger is essential both for the migrant himself and for the community upon which he is thrust. The migrant is unknown to us. We look upon the stranger with suspicion and upon all his habits and customs as queer and out of the ordinary. It is therefore natural for us to question his morality and character and to consider him the cause of the crimes and vices of the community. In the past, we blamed the Italians, the Slavs, the Jews and the other foreign groups as being mainly responsible for many of the anti-social acts in our urban society; but when we come to know them our attitude changes.

The Negro, although with us for centuries, is still unintelligible to the average northern community. This has been borne out by our present survey in the Pittsburgh district. Although in many instances the Negroes live near the whites, even among them, there is very little understanding or communication between the two races, and mutual prejudice and suspicion prevail.

With the cessation of the white immigration incident to the war and the influx of thousands of Negroes from the South the black has become the stranger in town. We see him crowding in certain districts, congregating on street corners, apparently amazed at his sudden transference from country to city life; from his home, a familiar though oppressive environment, into the glare and lure of the great industrial city with its apparent freedom for all. The Negro looks with wonder upon all this, and his reaction to it seems suspicious to the whites. When they see the police patrol wagon frequently in the colored district or when some crime is committed in that neighborhood it is not unnatural for them to think that these strangers are responsible for all crime and vice. This, unfortunately, is not only the attitude of the average person unfamiliar with conditions, but is also the theory upon which the police officials

46

seem to proceed in their work. On one occasion when a murder was committed in the "Hill" district the police made wholesale arrests of the Negroes, only to free them in a few days, having no evidence against them.

This assumption of the Negro's responsibility for a "wave of crime, rape and murder" this year was held not only by persons who got their information from a played-up case in the newspapers, but also by many social workers and Negroes themselves, as was evidenced by their expressed personal opinions. A colored probation officer, for instance, asserted that the juvenile delinquency among her people had at least doubled during the last year, and she was greatly surprised when an examination of the records disclosed a very considerable decrease in these cases, (Table No. XIX). This illustrates how erroneous our impressions about strange groups in our communities may be, and how essential are the facts to a clear understanding of the situation.

Wednesday 3:30 P. M. Lower Wylie Avenue.

In order to ascertain the facts concerning the extent of Negro crime in the Pittsburgh district, an analysis was made of the police court records of seven months in the year 1914-1915 in comparison with the same period of 1916-1917. The periods selected were December 1, 1914 to June 30, 1915 and December 1, 1916 to June 30, 1917. The first period embraces the time of the initial war prosperity before the migration had begun. In the second period the Negro migration was at its highest point. The police dockets of Station Number 1, the Central Station, and Station Number 2—which is in the most densely populated Negro section of the city—were carefully canvassed and compared as to number of arrests, kind of charges, disposition of cases and age, sex, etc., of the accused. Tables follow:

47

TABLE NUMBER XV

*Showing Total Number of Charges of Arrested Negroes Brought
to Stations No. 1 and No. 2 from December 1, 1914 to
June 30, 1915 and December 1, 1916 to June 30, 1917, and
also the percentage of Increase during the last Period.*

CHARGES	1914-1915			1916-1917			% of Inc. 1917
	Male	Female	Total	Male	Female	Total	
PETTY OFFENCES							
Suspicious Persons	390	77	467	668	111	779	67
Disorderly Conduct	353	74	427	493	106	599	41
Drunkenness	240	42	282	869	40	909	222
Keeping Disorderly Houses	16	22	38	36	55	91	140
Visiting Disorderly Houses	92	29	121	217	76	293	142
Common Prostitute	0	58	58	0	54	54	—7
Violating City Ordinances	85	0	85	143	0	143	68
Keeping Gambling Houses	5	0	5	0	0	0	
Visiting Gambling Houses	31	0	31	0	0	0	
Vagrancy	75	9	84	93	0	93	11
Other non-Court Charges	83	0	83	37	0	37	
TOTAL	1370	311	1681	2556	442	2998	
MAJOR OFFENCES							
Larceny	20	1	21	20	3	23	
Assault & Battery	12	0	12	13	0	13	
Highway Robbery	3	0	3	4	0	4	
Entering Buildings	20	0	20	7	0	7	
Felonious Cutting & Felonious Shooting	7	1	8	17	2	19	
Murder turned over to Coroner	12	0	12	5	1	6	
Assault and Battery with attempt to Commit Rape	5	0	5	3	0	3	
Concealed Weapons & Point. Firearms	2	1	3	12	0	12	
Other Court Charges	9	0	9	6	1	7	
TOTAL	90	3	93	87	7	94	
GRAND TOTAL	1460	314	1774	2643	449	3092	

The foregoing tables and figures reveal many features which are extremely interesting. The first thing that strikes us is the disproportionate increase in petty arrests over the increase in court charges or graver crimes. From the figures obtained it appears that although the number of arrests on charges of suspicion, drunkenness, disorderly conduct and similar petty charges have increased from approximately forty percent to over two hundred percent; the graver crimes, as a whole, have remained stable in spite of the increase in population, while in some of the crimes which are usually accredited to Negroes, we find a marked decline. The percentage of grave charges compared to the total number of arrests, has decreased from 5% in 1914-15 to 3% in 1916-17. Thus, we find only two more larcenies in 1916-17 than in 1914-15; a considerable decline in charges for entering buildings and two charges less of rape.

TABLE NUMBER XVI

Showing the disposition of the Negroes Arrested and Brought to Police Stations Number 1 and Number 2 from December 1, 1914 to June 30, 1915 and December 1, 1916 to June 30, 1917; the percentage of the total arrests and the percentage of increase or decrease during the latter period.

DISPOSITION	1914-15 Total No.	1916-17 Total No.	Percentage of Total Arrests 1914-15	1916-17	% of inc.	% of dec.
Discharged	849	1716	48	55	102	
Held for Court	93	94	5	3	0	
Fines	308	532	17	17	73	
Jail	230	369	13	12	60	
Workhouse	179	334	10	11	87	
Otherwise disposed	114	47	7	2		
	1773	3092	100	100		

Of the three thousand ninety-two arrests during 1916-1917, one thousand seven hundred and sixteen were discharged without fines, again demonsrating the petty character or the lack of evidence on these charges.

It is not difficult to find an explanation for the tremendous increase in arrests on charges of suspicion, disorderly conduct and the like. The colored migrant, timid, friendless and unknown as he is when he comes from the South, easily becomes an object of surveillance. The railroads were bringing a train load of black workers practically every day. Many come to Pittsburgh with the desire to remain here, but the labor agents want them to go further east. Workers of this class either try to get away from the labor agent, or, being separated from him in the general confusion prevailing at the stations, are stranded and left without resources. As strangers they know nothing about the city or its ways. They are but lately come out from communities where they have known only oppression, and in many cases their exodus has been a secret one. It is not remarkable that men in their state of mind should be looked upon by the police as questionable characters and arrested on the charges of being suspicious persons, or should fall into the hands of the law for various other reasons.

The marked increase in drunkenness is not surprising either. From an analysis of the housing and lodging situation in Pittsburgh the reader will realize that these migrants have no place in which to spend their leisure time except the street corners and in the saloon. In practically all rooming houses beds are run on a double shift basis. A man may stay in his room only when he sleeps. On awakening he must surrender his bed to another lodger and go elsewhere. There are no recreational facilities provided him by the city. Only one place, the saloon, welcomes him with open doors, and even this danger-ous hospitality is denied him except in the Negro quarters. That the stranger should not embrace the only means of relaxation offered him in his new environment would be incredible.

TABLE NUMBER XVII

Showing the age and sex of the persons Arrested in the two Stations from December 1, 1914 to June 30, 1915 and from December 1, 1916 to June 30, 1917.

	Total No. 1914-15		Total 1916-17		Total 1914-15	1916-17
	Male	Female	Male	Female		
Under 16	40	8	21	7	48	28
16 to 20	69	31	112	18	100	130
20 to 30	556	195	1133	237	751	1370
30 to 40	398	109	797	96	507	893
40 to 50	232	18	432	35	250	467
50 and over	107	11	192	12	118	204
	1402	372	2687	405	1774	3092

TABLE NUMBER XVIII

Showing the Number of Married and Single People Arrested;
Also Showing the Sex.

| | Total No. 1914-15 | | Total No. 1916-17 | | TOTAL | |
	Male	Female	Male	Female	1914-15	1916-17
Single	1024	194	2269	256	1218	2525
Married	395	161	428	139	556	567
	1419	355	2697	395	1774	3092

That there should be a big increase in the visitation of disorderly houses is to be expected. As we have seen, the migration is as yet largely that of single men and of men who have left their families behind them. As with the other foreign groups who have migrated to America, there is an entire break up of the normal family standard. It is therefore inevitable that with higher wages and with the prevailing housing and rooming congestion vice should flourish. The fact that in spite of the tremendous increase in disorderly houses there is some decline in arrests on charges of prostitution can be interpreted only in terms of the laxity and tolerance of the police department. This also accounts for the fact that while during the seven months of 1914-1915 five gambling houses were raided and thirty-one persons were arrested for gambling, there were no raids or arrests during the same period this year.

The big increase in arrests on charges of felonious cutting, pointing firearms, and carrying concealed weapons, may be explained in a variety of ways. Since the post bellum days, the carrying and handling of arms in the South was sanctioned socially. The whites have carried, and in some places are still carrying these weapons with them. The Negro, whether because of his habit of imitating the whites or because he has learned the lesson of protecting and defending himself, has also acquired the habit of carrying weapons. Being too poor or too timid in the South to purchase a revolver or similar dangerous weapon, he had to contend himself with a knife or a razor.

Immediately upon the Negro's arrival in Pittsburgh, and as soon as he gets off the train, his attention is called to these means of defense which are profusely displayed in the show windows of second hand stores near the stations. These arms are tempting to his primitive instinct of display, and being unfamiliar with conditions in this city—still thinking in terms of the Southern environment—he considers these things a necessity. As they can be obtained easily, he manages to purchase one of these weapons at the first opportunity. That the lynchings, riots and mistreatments should not teach him a lesson of self-defense and the need for such weapons would be incredible. It may also be added that the Southern Negro does not consider cutting another Negro an offense against the law. Such cutting was frequently practiced in the South and arrest did not follow. It may therefore not be strange to learn that on several occasions, when arraigned on charges of felonious cutting, these migrants expressed great surprise when they learned that their offense involved a jail or workhouse sentence.

TABLE NUMBER XIX

Total Number of Negro Charges in the Juevnile Court from January 1st, 1915 to June 30, 1915 and January 1st, 1917 to June 30, 1917.

CHARGES	Total No. 1915	Total No. 1917
Incorrigibility	11	10
Delinquency	34	13
Dependent and Neglected	18	23
Entering a Building	4	1
Larceny	5	8
Violating Parole	1	0
Malicious Mischief	2	1
Assault and Battery	5	1
All other Charges	3	3
	83	60

TABLE NUMBER XX

Dispositions of Same.

Returned to Parents	3	4
Detention Home	1	0
Private Home	30	15
Home on Probation	22	16
Thorn Hill Industrial School	15	12
State Reformatory	4	2
Polk School for Feeble Minded	1	5
Other Places	7	6
	83	60

Table number XVII indicates that the majority of those arrested are between the ages of 20 and 40. The large number of women arrested is rather surprising, although the proportional increase of women arrested is far below that of men. This may be due to the fact that the migration is largely of men without families. The overwhelming number of single people as compared with married ones, is also to be expected, although the police record based only upon uninvestigated statements of prisoners, may not be very authentic.

A House in the Hill District Credited with Sheltering Over 200 Negroes.

The examination of police court dockets reveals one or two other significant features. It shows the continuance of the migration by the fact that a great number are listed as having "no homes." The number giving such "address" this year is far greater than during the previous period; even when the total of those who refuse to give correct addresses is subtracted, the increase is still clearly shown. In the records of those who give their addresses as of this city, it is important to note the close relation of congestion and bad housing conditions to the police court records. Throughout the docket, a few houses notorious for their overcrowding stand out very prominently. Thus, a well known tenement house on Bedford Avenue, which is credited with having over one hundred families inside its four walls, has given eighty-four arrests during the seven months of 1914-1915, and over one hundred during the seven months of 1917. The same thing is true of several other houses.

53

Table number **XIX** showing the Juvenile Court records is surprising. That there should still be an absolute decline in juvenile delinquency, in spite of the increase in population, is something the most optomistic of us would have hardly anticipated.

After the proceeding analysis, the reader has doubtless already realized how unfounded was the popular belief in a Negro "wave of crime, rape and murder" in Pittsburgh within the last year. The facts are self-evident. From our analysis, we must conclude that the Negro migrant is not a vicious character; is not criminally and mischievously inclined *per se*, but on the other hand is a peaceful and law abiding individual. He comes to Pittsburgh to seek better economic and social opportunities. He is in most instances anxious to let others alone in order that he himself may be let alone.

That the rise in wages is a considerable factor in the decrease of juvenile delinquency and graver crimes as a whole is probable. That the Negro becomes a victim of the saloon and the vice elements is evidently more the fault of the community than of himself. He is often anxious to rid himself of these associations, but it can be done only by his white brother's realization of the social responsibility which he owes to the community.

HEALTH STUDY

That the conservation of health is no longer the concern of the individual affected alone, but is the problem of the whole community is now generally recognized. The relation of cause and effect in our complex urban life is nowhere more clearly shown than in the health phase of our group relations. In this aspect of community life at least, it is realized that each of us constitutes one of the cogs in the civic machinery, and that the welfare of the whole depends upon the welfare of the individual. No one in the city, even if he be living under the best conditions can be certain of immunity from the menace of epidemic or of venereal diseases and tuberculosis. Infantile paralysis, and the other contagious or infectious diseases have no regard for differences of social status or residential respectability.

The Negroes of Pittsburgh constitute a very considerable fraction of the city population. We have only partially segregated districts, and the Negroes live near us or in our midst. They are with us on the streets, in street cars, stores and amusement places. They work side by side with us in the mills, factories and offices. Their children and ours attend the same schools, drink from the same fountains and play in the same yards. Since the beginning of the European War, our foreign supply of domestic servants has been practically cut off, and the colored women are the only ones available for this type of work. These women live in our homes, wash our clothes, cook our dinners, make our beds and nurse our children. A close inter-relation between the two races exists, and we cannot long hope to be free from the diseases to which our servants are subject. Once it is realized that our own welfare is greatly affected by the welfare of the Negro, it is obvious that we must see to it that his health is conserved. Our old ostrich-like policy of comfortable neglect will not serve to protect us.

INTERIOR COURT SCENE
Note Hydrant on Left and Privy on Right which are used by Twelve Families, White and Negro.

We cannot remain indifferent to the startling adult and infant mortality rates among Negroes. Ignorance of and indifference to disease in any one group will ultimately work harm to the entire population, and neglected disease in the black race means the increase of disease among the whites. It is essential, therefore, for our own well being that we look into the conditions under which our Negro brethren live; and ascertain all the facts which may throw some light upon the actual conditions existing. Hence, we have proceeded to analyze the records which could be obtained in our city health

55

department, the records of a few of the larger hospitals in the
city, and the records of the coroner's office. The tables and
discussion of the same follow.

It is unfortunate that the statistical bureau of our Health
Department—whether through insufficient appropriations or
otherwise—does not maintain the standards set by similar departments in other cities. Our department does not afford the
information necessary for a complete study of the health situation. However, from the figures obtained, it is obvious that
our Negro mortality rate and especially the infant mortality
rate is much higher than that of New York City, for instance,
and that we are facing a grave situation.

TABLE NUMBER XXI

*Causes of the Negro Mortality Comparing Periods of Seven
Months, January to July, 1915 and January
to July, 1917.*

CAUSES	1915	1917
Pneumonia (all forms)	64	183
Tuberculosis (all forms)	51	51
Bright's Disease and Nephritis	21	23
Apoplexy	9	20
Meningitis	1	17
Syphilis	12	6
Heart Disease	23	45
Diabetes	4	5
Cancer (all forms)	9	8
Bronchitis (all forms)	4	9
Scarlet Fever	2	1
Whooping Cough	1	1
Diphtheria	1	2
Typhoid Fever	2	5
Measles	3	0
Poleomelitis	0	2
Peritonitis	0	5
Rickets	5	1
Puerperal Septicaemia	1	4
Uremia	0	4
Asphyxia	0	6
Cirrhosis of Liver	2	0
Accidents	12	16
Homicide	8	3
All other causes	60	110
	295	527

From a glance at the Negro mortality figures in Pittsburgh during the first seven months of 1917, (Table No. XXI), we observe the startling total of five hundred and twenty-seven deaths (excluding still births) as compared with two hundred and ninety-five deaths in 1915 during the anti-migration period, an increase of seventy-eight percent. While it is true that the Negro population has increased according to our estimate about forty-five percent during the past two years, this expansion in nowise explains the disquieting increase in mortality. An examination of the table also reveals the character of this increase. Pneumonia cases have increased nearly two hundred percent; we also had a marked increase in acute bronchitis and meningitis, and almost twice as many deaths from heart disease.

It is often claimed that the Negro is affected by climatic changes. Transferred suddenly into a northern climate, and compelled to live in all sorts of dwellings, often with no ventilation and light and in congested quarters, he may easily succumb to disease. Unaccustomed as he is to the heavy labor and pace-setting of the Pittsburgh industries, it can readily be seen how rapidly his health is undermined through excessive and hard labor. The fact that there has been no increase in tuberculosis is in accord with the expressed opinion of many colored physicians interviewed, who claimed that this disease is mainly a city product, and that the new-comers, especially those coming from isolated southern districts, are apt to be relatively free from this disease for a considerable period after their arrival in Pittsburgh.

TABLE NUMBER XXII

Record of Negro Morbidity for a Period of Six Months Before the Migration, as Compared with an Equal Period during the Migration in the West Penn Mercy and St. Francis Hospitals.

CAUSES	1915	1917
Digestive System	24	29
Respiratory and Throat	54	76
Heart and Kidney	16	10
Brain and Nervous System	9	5
Urogenital Diseases	35	44
	138	164

Table number XXII was ascertained from a study of the records of three of the largest hospitals in Pittsburgh, as to the treatment of Negro patients in these Institutions for a period of six months before the migration and an equal period during the migration. Although this table proved interesting, as showing the amount, kind and extent of the hospital morbidity among the colored people, it is not at all conclusive. That the hospital records give no clue to the sickness among the Negroes is apparent from the following: Eighty to ninety percent of the hospital cases examined were ward patients. Very few Negroes can afford private rooms, and almost every colored physician complained of the difficulty he had in securing places for his patients. It is only fair to state however, that one of the largest hospitals in the city, had no such charge lodged against it.

Aside from possible difficulty in securing beds in the hospitals, there is another cause for the scanty number of Negro hospital cases. The Negro not only because of his ignorance, but perhaps even more because of his inclinations to voodooism and superstition, feels an aversion to the hospital, where he thinks the knife and the "black bottle" are frequently used. He is still childlike in many ways, and will prefer all sorts of patent medicines and quack doctors rather than expose himself to the surgeon's knife in a hospital; and chooses to stay at home among his own people where he may "die in peace."

TABLE NUMBER XXIII

Comparative Record of the Births and Deaths of Negroes and the Entire City Population, during the Year of 1915 and the First Seven Months of 1917.

NEGRO		ENTIRE CITY	
1915		**1915**	
BIRTHS	565	BIRTHS	16,139
DEATHS	536	DEATHS	8,722
FIRST SEVEN MONTHS 1917		**FIRST SEVEN MONTHS 1917**	
BIRTHS	356	BIRTHS	11,013
DEATHS	527	DEATHS	7,657

There is no more striking phase of the local Negro problem, than that shown in table number XXIII. These figures disclose the astonishing fact that the death rate among Negroes in this city during the first seven months of 1917, was forty-eight percent greater than the birth rate. In other words, while in the city population as a whole, the number of deaths was thirty percent less than the number of births, the num-

58

ber of deaths among colored people was forty-eight percent more than the number of births; thus, for every one hundred persons born in Pittsburgh in 1917, there were seventy deaths, while among the colored population, for every one hundred children born, one hundred and forty-eight persons died.

These figures seem of sinister significance to the Negro race. Even when taking into consideration the facts that the migration is largely that of single males, rather than that of families, and that because most of the women here are doing some work outside the home there is a definite policy of limiting their birth rate, there still remains the fact that even during the entire year of 1915, while the birth rate of the entire city population was practically twice the death rate, the excess number of births over deaths among colored people was only twenty-nine in a total of over five hundred.

TABLE NUMBER XXIV

Ages of Persons who Died Within the First Seven Months of 1917.

Under 1 year	87
Under 5 years	43
From 5 to 12	16
From 12 to 20	24
From 20 to 30	69
From 30 to 40	101
From 40 to 60	138
Over 60	49
TOTAL	527

TABLE NUMBER XXV

Causes of Deaths of Children Under 5 Years of Age.

Burns	1	Influenza	2
Malnutrition	4	Asphyxia	4
Syphilis	4	Hemorrhage	1
Tuberculosis Meningitis	3	Convulsions	6
Pneumonia	51	Diphtheria	2
Tuberculosis	5	Rickets	1
Enteritis	2!	Heart Disease	8
Premature	9	Mumps	1
Meningitis	2	Poliomelitis	1
Bronchitis	4	TOTAL	130

That the infant mortality rate among colored people is much higher than among the white groups, is generally believed and it is not surprising to find that the mortality among Negro infants in Pittsburgh is much greater than the infant mortality rate for the entire city. Figures for the year 1916-17 were unobtainable. The records of the Department of Health show that during the year 1915 one hundred and four children per thousand born in Pittsburgh, died in their first year.

There were three hundred and fifty-six Negro births in the first seven months of 1917. During the same period eighty-seven Negro children died under one year. Of this number fifty-nine had been born between January and July 1917, which means that one hundred and sixty-six children per thousand die in their first seven months. This clearly indicates that the death rate of Negro infants is far above the death rate of white infants. Table No. XXV also shows the cause of deaths of children under five years of age who died within the last seven months. At least half of these deaths were due to preventable disorders, as is apparent from the figures in the same table.

TABLE NUMBER XXVI

Colored Bodies Received and Disposed of in Morgue, First Six Months During 1915 as Compared with First Six Months During 1917.

	1915	1917	TOTAL
Identified and Claimed	13	32	45
Identified and Cremated	5	13	18
Unknown and Cremated	1	2	3
	19	47	66

The figures obtained from the Coroner's Office also indicate an abnormal increase in the number of colored bodies received and disposed of by the County Morgue. There were more than twice as many morgue cases within the first six months of 1917 as during the same period of 1915. That the majority of these bodies were claimed and not disposed of at public expense, is doubtless due to the high wages paid this year. High wages at least provide for burials, which are considered of paramount importance by the Negroes, because of their primitive superstition, and abhorrence of having their bodies turned over for the purpose of dissection.

The proceeding analysis indicates that the conservation of the health of the Negro in Pittsburgh is a very complex problem, and is inter-related with his social, moral, industrial, housing and racial situation. The Negro is affected by all the elements which render difficult the preservation of health among whites but in a greater degree. Many of the factors which work continuously to undermine his health are to a large extent eliminated among whites; and on the other hand, much of the effective work done by whites to counteract these bad influences is entirely lacking among Negroes.

"The Triad of 'baby-killers'—poverty, ignorance and neglect"—says Dr. Sobel, of the New York Health Department, "works havoc among Negro children to a greater extent even than among the whites."

"The well-known relationship between family income and infant mortality exists among Negroes as among the whites. The crude death rate is exceedingly high in all Negro districts. There are, however, well-defined differences in their respective rates, resulting, we think, from economic conditions. In the districts where the family income is highest, the death rate is lowest, confirming the opinion that if we can improve the social and economic condition of the Negro, an appreciable reduction in their death rate will have been secured." (August, 1917 Bulletin of the Department of Health, New York City, pages 87 and 88.)

While we may admit the claim often advanced that even under the same conditions disease and infant mortality among Negroes would ordinarily be higher than that of the whites, because, due to the climatic and environmental maladjustments, his racial power of resistence is not as great as that of the white; the Negro is still confronted with many forces which handicap and work against him, but which are almost non-existent among the whites.

From our discussion of employment, housing and opportunities for advancement in Pittsburgh, the reader will realize the difficulties and hardships which the Negro is compelled to face in this city. Only a very few of the Negro migrants earn more than $3.60 a day for twelve hours work. Half of the families here live in one room dwellings. Practically all of the mothers are doing some work outside the home. The Negroes have as yet no organization for mutual cooperation. They live separate and apart from each other. In many cases

61

for instance, it was found in our survey, that women living next door to each other for months would hardly know one another, although often they would both come from the same state and even from the same city. The Negroes are more exposed and liable to disease because their social, industrial, educational and moral development is more handicapped than that of the white man. The Negro is apparently as yet not free even in the North; he is still held captive in economic bondage, and is deterred from rising above the lowest servant class. He is, judging from the present situation, limited to common labor at thirty cents an hour during prosperous times.

The conservation of health, is as we have seen, no longer the problem of the individual. It is therefore time that we awaken to the realization that sickness and a high mortality rate among Negroes is no longer the problem of the Negro alone. Eventually all of us will have to pay the price for our indifference, both in money and in lives. The taxpayer ultimately pays for hospitals and morgues, as well as for jails and prisons. Our children are not at all immune from the sources of disease which are ravaging the colored children. This problem is our problem; we must face it squarely, and see whether any improvement in this situation is possible.

The significance of such a study and its importance as the basis for a practical program is clearly demonstrated by the remarkable results brought about in New York City through a similar study. After a survey of conditions in the Columbus Hill District, the Negro section of the Borough of Manhattan the startling evidence of conditions prevailing there stimulated the New York Bureau of Child Hygiene to take action. This Bureau has succeeded in reducing the infant mortality rate among colored people from 202 deaths per thousand children born in 1915 to 193.3 in 1916, and to 180 per thousand children born during the first six months of 1917.

Dr. Jacob Sobel, Chief of the Division of Baby Welfare, writes as follows in one of the recent monthly bulletins of the New York Department of Health.*

"The stimulus to our program was given by a study of conditions in the Columbus Hill District, and it was here that our efforts were first concentrated. It was our knowledge of the conditions in this district which led to an effort on the part of the Bureau of Child Hygiene to institute a campaign against the excessive death rate among colored infants, by studying primarily the needs of the situation, and by securing the co-

*August, 1917 Bulletin of the Department of Health, New York City.

operation of all agencies and individuals interested in the welfare of colored people. With this end in view, there was first instituted a preliminary census of the babies residing in the above district, by house to house canvas, and an effort was made to have these babies enrolled at the Baby Health Station within said district. Mothers' meetings were held at schools, settlement houses, churches, etc., at which the physicians of the Health Department gave short talks to the parents of the neighborhood. The co-operation of prominent colored citizens, ministers, physicians, newspaper men, etc., of the district, was secured. Educational slides, containing pointed references to the high mortality among colored babies, and special reference to the high mortality in particular sections inhabited by colored people, were prepared and displayed on the screens of the various moving picture houses in this and other districts.

"A series of articles on baby care was published in one of the newspapers read largely by the colored race, namely, 'The Amsterdam News', under the title of 'The Baby', and presented short heart-to-heart talks on baby care. The Department of Health also published a local bulletin for this district, known as 'The Columbus Hill Chronicle', in which special attention was directed to conditions among the colored population, with specific recommendations for the improvement of their health and surroundings.

"In view of the large number of working mothers among the colored people, a temporary shelter or day nursery for colored babies was established in this district through the cooperation of the Babies' Welfare Association, and funds have subsequently been provided, through private means, for the permanent equipment and maintenance, in the heart of this district, of a day nursery for colored children.

"The 'Little Mothers' of this district was organized, and in this way a large amount of education was brought into the homes.

"Immediately upon the receipt of notification of births in this and other colored districts, the Bureau of Records notified the Baby Health Station, in order that the home might be visited, and the infant enrolled for care and treatment.

"Special attention was directed to the supervision of colored babies boarded out in the homes, and wherever a colored baby was found, not a relative of the occupant of the premises, information was elicited whether this individual had a permit to board and care for a baby, as required by the provisions of the Sanitary Code.

"Provision was made for the distribution of free milk and free ice, to needy families of the districts, through the organized relief agencies and ice companies.

"Special attention was directed towards securing employment for the fathers, so as to keep the mothers at home as much as possible.

"To supplement the work of baby care, two nurses were assigned by the Department of Health to the Columbus Hill and Upper Harlem Districts, for instruction and supervision of expectant mothers. The Association for Improving the Condition of the Poor also assigned a nurse to the Columbus Hill District for similar instruction, so that a beginning was made to bring the colored expectant mother under the guiding influence of trained nurses.

"The cooperation of the Tenement House Department was affected to the extent that special attention was given to the sanitary condition of the tenements occupied by colored people.

"In a further effort to control the mortality among the colored babies, the policy of the Bureau to assign nurses during the summer months to those districts of the city showing a high infant mortality rate and a high birth rate, was applied with special reference to the colored sections, and a large force was assigned there, each nurse having under her direct charge from 100 to 150 babies during these months, keeping up this complement whenever, through death or removal, the number fell below the required amount."

It is inevitable with any group, suddenly transferred into a new situation, that striking maladjustments should arise. While single instances of suffering very often are misleading and do not give a just view of the case, numerous and typical incidents which are by no means exceptional or exaggerated may help to visualize the problem.

A Georgia farmer who is making $3.60 a day for twelve hours of work here brought over his wife and eight children, the oldest of whom was thirteen years of age, to a house which he was fortunate to secure on Second Avenue. Only a few weeks after his arrival all of the eight children were taken sick, and two of them, one eleven and the other six years old, died of pneumonia. Because of the contagion of some of his children the man was unable to leave his house for eight weeks. His physician said that the death of the children was due to the over-crowded condition of the house. This man received no charity and the money he had saved up was spent to the last cent on doctor bills.

Mrs. E. H. lives on Crawford Street with her three children the oldest of whom is five years of age. She occupies a small and damp room. Since there is no gas in the house, a red hot stove can always be found burning in the room which is at the same time kitchen, dining room, bedroom and washroom; for Mrs. H's husband is in jail somewhere in Georgia, and she does washing all day in order to support her children. The water supply of the house is in the street, and the stairway leading to the upper floors is in her room. All of her children were sick; one had pneumonia. She came here a few months ago as everybody else was coming. Relatives and charity are helping to support her.

Mr. F. J. P. was born in Jamaica of well-to-do parents, tobacco planters, and was educated in England as a botanist. He works now as a common laborer in Pittsburgh for he cannot secure work in his own field; he is planning to go back to England.

Mr. J. D. has had his wife here for several months, but still has his only child back in Florida as there is no room for him in his present place.

Messrs. E. and R. Smith, one living on Penn Avenue, and the other on Ross Street, worked for a steel plant and construction company respectively. E. had an eye accident and was in the hospital for four weeks, while R. had two fingers cut off while at work. The companies paid the hospital bills for both but neither one of them ever heard or knew anything about compensation, and never claimed any.

J. G. hails from West Virginia. He has been in town for two days and has no room as yet. The lodging places he went to asked seventy-five cents a night for a dirty bed. He stayed up both nights, and expects to leave the city as soon as he can.

The Case family have eight children. The oldest is a girl of seventeen years of age who works in a hotel. The mother works every day in the week; she leaves home at seven in the morning and returns at five o'clock in the afternoon. A girl of fifteen takes care of the children in the meantime.

Mr. P. Roberts was a prosperous Negro in Florida. He was an experienced concrete maker, earning according to his statement more than five and six dollars a day at home, and owning property in the South. When the industrial boom began he thought that the wages in his line were much higher here than in his own home town, and that it would pay him to come North. He came to Pittsburgh together with his wife, five children and an old invalid mother who was confined to bed. When first

65

visited, Mr. Roberts occupied two small rooms, each having one window, in a rooming house where there were about twenty-five male roomers. This man could get no work here in his own trade, and was trying to save up enough money from his $3.00 to $3.60 a day to go back to Florida. When Roberts was visited again about six weeks after the first visit, his old mother had already passed away, his wife had died of pneumonia, while his oldest girl of sixteen who had been taking care of the four little tots was sick in bed, and the children were playing on the streets. Roberts was still trying to save from his $3.60 a day sufficient money to carry him back to Florida, which he still considers his home, as he owns property there.

These amazing instances of individual maladjustments are bound to arise in any group which goes through such a sudden and abnormal transformation. But they are even more frequent in the race which is still primitive and child-like in many ways, with no one to direct, guide and protect them.

But the significance and danger of these wrongs are even of greater importance for the community as a whole, than for the few individuals affected. The fact cannot be over-emphasized that the community ultimately pays the price for its stupidity. Indifference to this problem at present when it still can be coped with and adjusted will result in an uncontrolable situation later. We have seen above some of the costly results of our housing and wage conditions. We have also learned in this war that we can no longer afford to breed and foment discontent and antagonism among our own people. We must not only see that the strangers among us are adjusted, but that they also do not become a menace to the well-being of the community.

It is not sufficient that we bring these people here, give them a "bunk-house" or a basement to sleep in, and a job in our mills for twelve hours a day. Once these people are in our midst they become a part of ourselves, and if we desire them to work in harmony with our own interests and not become anti-social malcontents we must go further than that. We must see that they become part and parcel of our community, that they are educated and made familiar with the problems that we are facing locally. The man who is here for several days and stays up all night because he can find no place to sleep cannot be expected to remain for long a social being. Pittsburgh's progress will be greatly handicapped if a certain element of our community has to take advantage of the saloon and vice resorts for relaxation. Neither can we afford to let a considerable part of our voting population remain, because of lack of intelligence, the prey and spoil of politicians who may jeopardize the whole life of the city for their own selfish interest. We cannot permit sickness and high mortality rates among the dark-skinned people. One of our big steel mills had to have its whole office and plant forces vaccinated, and was even in danger of being quarantined, when a number of Negroes working in the plant scattered all over the city after a case of smallpox was discovered in the rooming house where these men stopped. The Department of Health had a big task hunting these men, and the danger to which the whole city population was exposed was obvious. No more can we afford to let the Negroes become the victims of all sorts of anti-social elements and feel complacent after we send them for a period of time to the jail or workhouse. They are a heavy burden upon the taxpayer while they are in these Institutions and often become even a greater menace when they are released. Our utmost attention is therefore essential to meet the maladjustments before they have become acute; and we do not base this claim upon sentimental grounds but upon the benefits of economic and social far-sightedness.

Many Negroes in the North seem to understand the situation, and are striving to do their best to help adjust conditions. Some of the Negro churches in this city for instance tried to ameliorate the housing conditions by converting their churches into lodging places for the new-comers until rooms could be found for them. Besides the Provident Rescue Mission on Fullerton Street, which accommodated thirty to forty men at a time during the entire winter, at least one other church converted the entire building into quarters for migrant families. The latter church accommodated a number of families until the committee in charge could secure homes for the newcomers. But the responsibility of the white people is just as great, and it is indeed in very opportune time that a prophetic warning is sounded by a colored writer in a Cleveland paper as follows:

"Let them alone—permit them to grope blindly through the mazes of startling new environments, and in a few years a social problem will be created that will require a half century and millions of dollars to solve."

"Let them alone now, permit and enforce them to live in unsanitary districts and homes, relieved of Christian and moral influence, and what is perhaps a 20,000 responsibility today, will become a 50,000 heavy, crime-breeding burden tomorrow."

"Let them alone today, permit them to become the flotsman and jetsam of neglect, or pernicious discrimination—such as they were in the South—and tomorrow, having inhaled a bit of Northern freedom, they may become a dark, sinister shadow falling athwart the white man's door."

"Let them alone today, permit them to be retired to overcrowded shacks and shanties where sanitation is an unuttered word, and tomorrow, contagions, arising from these congested, unsanitary shanties and shacks, will fly, like the black bat of night, over our fair city, and in its wake will stalk the gaunt form of Death, claiming thousands of our best white and Colored citizens as a debt paid for inaction."

CHAPTER IV.

Some Constructive Suggestions Looking Toward the Solution of a Race Problem Through Race Co-Operation.

It would indeed be presumptious on our part to attempt in this little study to solve the race problem. Our purpose was to present the facts as they actually exist and let the reader draw his own conclusions. However, a few suggestions looking to a constructive policy of meeting the need caused by the Negro migration in Pittsburgh may not be amiss.

The main problem of the Negro migrant in Pittsburgh, as the reader has already realized, is his social and industrial maladjustment, his lack of organization, and absence of intelligent guidance. The National League on Urban Conditions among Negroes is attempting to meet this need by acting as adjusting agency, guide, educator and organizer. This League is composed of white and colored men, whose aim is to secure cooperation among the races and to act as a social medium between the two peoples. Within the last year this League has established eighteen different branches in various cities. Each of these branches is headed by a trained Negro Social worker, who tries to get in touch with the migrants as soon as they arrive in the town, and through the cooperation of local social agencies and business officials, endeavors to put each man into the right place. The League acts as a socializing factor among the colored people with the aim of securing closer cooperation between the two races. The success of these branches is evidenced by the fact that in some cities the League's staff had to be increased three and four times the original number within the last year, and in some instances these branches were established at the invitation of Chambers of Commerce.

A representative of the League who has spent some time in studying the situation in Pittsburgh thinks that it is comparatively easy for the League's Secretary here to get in touch with the newcomers as soon as they arrive, and to endeavor to eliminate a great deal of the industrial maladjustment which is due to the ignorance of the newcomer. This can be done, he claims, through the cooperation of the more than forty colored newspapers in the South, through the various branches of the League, and through definite arrangements at the Railroad stations. By keeping in touch with the employers and industrial concerns, the local Secretary could also succeed in reducing the number of men who are misplaced and misfits in their present jobs.

Some suggestions as to the work the League could do in Pittsburgh, are thus outlined by the representative of the League.

"Besides the advertising in the newspapers, and the cooperation of the League's branches some Traveler's Aid work may be done as a result of the heavy Negro migration to Pittsburgh. Definite service might be arranged at the railroad stations for directing newcomers to reliable lodging houses, so as to protect them from unfavorable surroundings. Likewise aid from the police department can be sought to eliminate a large number of crooks and gamblers who thrive off the earnings of newly arrived migrants in the congested sections.

"The industrial work is an essential part of our program, including general employment, opening new opportunities and vocational guidance. An important part of this work will be with the industrial plants employing large numbers of Negro migrants. The Secretary will make an especial effort to reduce the large Negro labor turnover in the various industrial plants by noon-day and Sunday talks, by distributing literature among the men and by assisting corporations in getting the most reliable type of Negro labor and then seeing to it that this labor is properly treated and given opportunities for advancement. Vagrancy must not be tolerated in Pittsburgh especially when work is so plentiful.

"The Housing work will be broad and cover both an effort to obtain more sanitary houses for Negroes to live in, as well as less congested, unhealthy and hence less immoral living conditions in certain parts of the city. The difficulties might be partially overcome by encouraging the organization of a Building and Loan Association and by interesting real estate dealers, builders and owners who handle or own property in desirable districts to improve the same for Negro tenants; by urging individual home ownership, and, with more chance of success in the Pittsburgh district, by convincing industries of the basic necessity for building family homes.

"Health and sanitation are of vital interest to Negroes and to Pittsburghers. One of the first efforts will be a campaign to reduce the high illness and death rates among the Negroes. In cooperation with the Bureau of Sanitation, physicians and Negro Institutions and Organizations, an educational campaign can be waged giving wide publicity to the facts obtained and suggesting remedies concerning,

a. The danger and use of patent medicines; b. Carelessness in dress; c. Improper ventilation; d. Care of infants, etc. Following this campaign a general effort may be made to clean up Negro neighborhoods, to obtain better and cleaner streets and sidewalks, better sanitary inspection, police service and if possible, a free bath house for the lower Hill district.

"The question of amusement and recreation is likewise important, as they have a direct bearing on good citizenship. Definite cooperation can be established with such existing organizations as the Y. M. C. A., Washington Park Playground, Settlements, and the churches which have the facilities for such work. Boy and girl clubs can be organized under capable leaders. A supervised community dance can do much toward helping the newcomer to better adjust themselves socially.

"Delinquency, especially juvenile crime, should be handled in connection with the courts, probation officers and schools; the League furnishing through its office Big Brothers and Sisters with the idea of organizing this work on a larger scale later on. The penal and reformatory institution serving the Community should be reached to help discharged and paroled prisoners to obtain a new start and be reclaimed for their own good and that of society.

"A very close relationship must exist between our charity and the organized charities, because our association does not provide for relief. An effort will be made to develop cooperation among welfare organizations already existing in the community, to prevent expensive duplication of work and to assure good feeling and harmony among workers.

"The details of this work may be reviewed from time to time by an executive committee, which should consist of from ten to fifteen persons chosen from the membership of the association."

APPENDIX

TABLE NUMBER XXVII

Increase in Number of Colored Children in the Schools of the Hill District from January to October 1917, *and Number of Children from Southern States Since January,* 1917.

NAME OF SCHOOL	Total Number of Colored Children		Children who Came from Southern States	% of Increase within the last 10 Months
	Jan.	Oct.		
Franklin	69	99	37	44
Miller	36	57	17	58
Madison	20	28	3	40
Moorhead	178	222	55	25
Minersville	181	271	97	50
Letsche	91	160	55	76
McKelvy	88	120	33	36
Somers	201	289	45	39
Watt	422	529	62	26
Rose	129	198	62	53
	1415	1973	466	

Total Average Increase 40%

Table number XXVII was compiled from the figures supplied by the principals of the eleven schools listed. These schools are located in the Hill District. The figures indicate the increase in the one section only, and do not include all the children who have been brought from the South, but whose parents reside in other sections of the city. The marked increase in the total number of colored children and the great increase in the number of children who have come to this city within the last ten months is significant.

As one would expect the majority of these children are in the lower four grades. This was the case even before the migration but is especially true since the migration. Many of the children from the South either had no schooling at all, or were attending schools with lower standards than ours.

The problem of over-aged pupils is very significant among the Negro children. A principal in one of these schools who has recently made a little study of over-aged pupils in these eleven schools finds that the percentage of Negro children eleven years and over in the lower four grades, is far greater than that of the whites (sixteen percent Negro as compared with four and seven tenths percent whites). This, the same principal remarks, is in spite of the fact that the tendency of the schools is often to promote children upon the basis of their size and age, rather than because of academic attainment. What is more the white children in most of these schools come from homes where the parents are not Americans, but foreigners who often do not speak the English language.

The causes for the backwardness of the Negro children are deep-lying, and are interlinked with their racial traits, social, economic and home environments. Practically all school principals stated that in the first four years the Negro child keeps well up with its white school mates, but that after the fourth grade, the Negro child often falls behind and cannot keep up with the whites.

It was apparent from our interviews with these principals that most of these men and women are quite alert and eager to find some means of remedying this difficult situation. Many of them have endeavored for a long time to cope with this problem, and a few think they have found ways to render more rapid progress of these children possible. But in the formal character of the school curriculum they have little freedom to develop their own schemes. These principals have practically all agreed that a system of motor-education which would emphasize the practical and industrial side rather than the purely academic, would not only benefit a large number of white children, but would prove absolutely invaluable for the colored children who, they believe, are more motor-minded than the whites. It would certainly, they think, solve the over-age problem to a large extent, and would make the chidren better prepared to avail themselves of the economic opportunities offered by our urban industrialism.

TABLE NUMBER XXVIII

Detailed Budget Study of Fifteen Families Including the Income and Expenditures for Seven Consecutive Days During the Month of September, 1917.

No. in Family	Family Income	Food	Clothing and Household ex. and carfare	Rents Per Week	Church	Medicine	Luxuries	Insurance
4	$25.25	$4.67	$2.85	$3.25	....	$0.86	$0.20	....
3	15.00	7.91	1.20	2.40	....	.50	.05	....
4	18.00	10.98	8.66	2.50	....	.40	.....	$0.45
3	28.50	6.38	9.29	2.50	$1.10	2.45	.30	....
2	17.00	3.77	19.60	2.10	....	.....	.....	....
3	18.00	10.25	4.05	2.00	....	.....	.33	.72
3	21.00	7.35	.30	3.50	....	.....	2.10	....
2	18.00	4.07	8.02	3.75	....	.25	.20	....
5	23.10	12.78	6.24	2.75	....	.....	1.60	1.50
3	18.50	4.12	26.65	2.00	....	.....	.....	....
2	15.00	8.43	1.24	4.25	....	.....	.05	....
2	16.50	9.51	....	3.00	....	.....	.20	.80
3	18.00	6.10	1.07	4.00	....	1.00	.....	....
5	17.00	13.17	3.00	3.00	....	.05	1.75	.25
5	14.00	7.87	2.48	6.00	.60	.....	.....	.65

Table number XXVIII is a study of the budgets of fifteen migrant families for seven consecutive days. The income includes the earnings of both husband and wife. The figures on the expenditures are approximately correct, although it was possible that in some families there were no big food expenditures the first day, and in other families food might have been left over after the seventh day.

The wide variation in the expenditures of these families on all the necessary articles is significant, and is probably indicative and typical of the maladjusted life and the diversity of the living conditions of the migrants. The wide variety of food expenditures is due primarily to the inordinate expenditures for meat, which in one or two instances reached over eight dollars per week. This is typical of the lack of balance of the diet.

The few cases of disproportionate expenditures on household goods were made by migrants who had bought some furniture for their new quarters. It is interesting to note, however, that these families were compelled to skimp

on their food, as their food bills are the lowest.   Under
luxuries we included all expenditures on tobacco, liquor, candy
and the like.   The few cases of considerable expenditures in this
column are due largely to the liquor bills.   The little use of
these articles in most families is apparent from the table. The
table as a whole, also, indicates the high cost of the living ne-
cessities of these migrants in Pittsburgh and their comparatively low wages.

TABLE NUMBER XXIX

*Negro Families Under Care of the Associated Charities with
Causes of Dependency During the Year Ending
September 30, 1917.*

1.	Unemployed	30
3.	Child Labor	1
4.	Work shyness	13
5.	Disalibity through industrial accident	2
6.	Tuberculosis	3
7.	Other sickness	34
8.	Blindness or sight seriously impaired	4
9.	Other physical handicap	1
10.	Feeble mindedness	2
11.	Epilepsy	1
12.	Insanity	1
13.	Other mental disease	5
14.	Old Age	10
15.	Death or burial	9
16.	Alcoholic intemperance	17
17.	Sexual irregularity	18
18.	Desertion or non-support	36
19.	Imprisonment	6
20.	Juvenile delinquency	11
21.	Abuse or neglect of children	32
22.	Debt	7
23.	Pauperized by unwise charity	2
24.	Hereditary pauperism	1
25.	Begging tendency	8
26.	Illegitimacy	7
27.	Domestic incompetency	10
28.	Illiteracy	3
29.	Domestic infelicity	1
30.	Bad housing.	25
31.	Non-adjusted immigrant	3
	Total	303

Schedule Used in Interviewing the Negro Migrants.

I (1) NAME   (2) Present Address   (3) Since   No.

(4) Age   (5) S. M. W.   (6) Health

(7) Occupation   (8) Employer   (9) Hours Daily   (10) Weekly Wage

(11) Kind of House   (12) Rooms in House   (13) Water Supply   (14) Toilet

(15) No. in House   (16) No. in Bedroom   (17) No. Beds   (18) No. Windows in Room

(19) How Does He   (20) Leisure Time

    Spend Money   (a) Church

    Weekly?   (b) Saloon

    (a) Room   (c)

    (b) Board

    (c) or Family   (21) Court Record

II (a) Former Address   (c) Last Employer   (d) Hours Daily

    (b) Former Occupations   (c) Weekly Wage

    (f)   Family   (g) Kind of Work   (b) Weekly

         (age)   Wage

W. 2   (i) Why Left Home?

Ch. 3   (j) Who Paid Carfare Here?

" 4   (k) Will Family Come Here?

" 5   (l) When?

" 6   (m) Live Where

" 7   (n) When Will He Go Back

" 8   (o) Why?

" 9

    Total Income

SIGNATURE   DATE